Red Cloud

FRANK H. GOODYEAR III

Red Cloud

Photographs of a Lakota Chief

University of Nebraska Press : Lincoln and London

Publication of this book was assisted by a grant from the Andrew W. Mellon Foundation.

Library of Congress Cataloging in Publication Data
Goodyear, Frank Henry, 1967–
Red Cloud : photographs of a Lakota chief / Frank H. Goodyear III.
p.cm. – (The Great Plains photography series)
Includes bibliographical references and index.
ISBN 0-8032-2192-4 (cloth : alkaline paper)
1. Red Cloud, 1821–1909. 2. Oglala Indians – Portraits. 3. Oglala
Indians – Kings and rulers – Pictorial works. I. Title. II. Series
E99.O3 G66 2003 978.004'9752'0092–dc21 [B] 2002075092

Contents

Acknowledgments

A number of wonderful individuals assisted me in the research and writing of this book. Their contributions had a profound impact on my thinking about this subject and my understanding of what it means to write history.

In looking for photographs of Red Cloud and conducting research into his life, I worked in more than two dozen different museums and archives across the United States. I am deeply appreciative of the many curators, librarians, archivists, registrars, and friends who helped me during this time. In particular, I thank Paula Fleming, National Anthropological Archives; Joanna Cohan Scherer, Handbook of the North American Indians; George Horse Capture and Emil Her Many Horses, National Museum of the American Indian; William Truettner, Smithsonian American Art Museum; Ann Shumard and Dru Dowdy, National Portrait Gallery; Jennifer Brathvode, Library of Congress; John Carter and Jill Koelling, Nebraska State Historical Society; LaVera Rose, South Dakota State Historical Society; Jennifer Thom, Denver Public Library; Barbara McCandless and Courtney DeAngelis, Amon Carter Museum; Barbara Narendra and Roger Colten, Peabody Museum of Natural History, Yale University; Barbara Landis, Cumberland County Historical Society; Janet Ness, University of Washington Special Collections; Mark Hertig, Agate Fossil Beds National Monument; Brother Simon, Red Cloud Indian School Heritage Center; Belle Lecher, Dawes County Historical Society; Julie Lakota, Oglala Lakota College; Neil O'Donnell, Buffalo-Erie County Historical Society; Jordan Rockford, Historical Society of Pennsylvania; Elizabeth Holmes, Buffalo Bill Historical Center; Melissa Wolfe, Columbus Art Museum; William Goetzmann and Ron Tyler, University of Texas at Austin; Erika Doss, University of Colorado at Boulder; Peter Nabokov, University of California at Los Angeles; Raymond Bucko, Creighton University; Robert Larson, University of Northern Colorado; and the editors and staff at the University of Nebraska Press. And special thanks go to Dorene Red Cloud, Bernard Red Cloud, Don Tenoso, and Charles Trimble.

Let me also acknowledge the love and support of my family. To Mom and Dad, Alison and Charlie, Grace and Adam, Aunt Alison and Uncle Bill, and my dear grandparents: thank you so much. And to my wife Anne: you have been a best friend throughout this long project.

Red Cloud

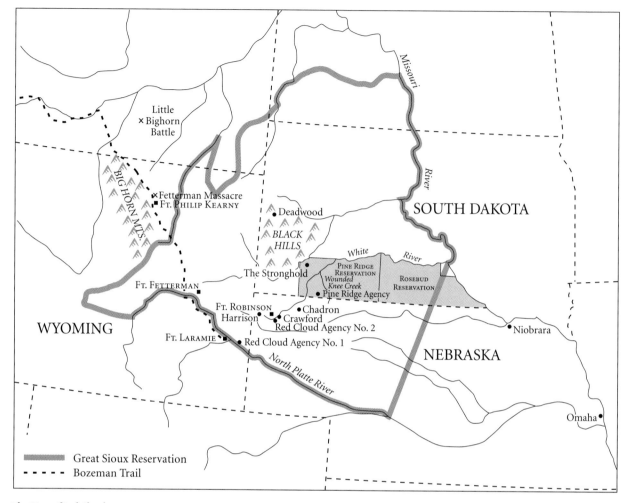

Little
×Bighorn
Battle

BIG HORN MTS.

× Fetterman Massacre
■ Ft. Philip Kearny

● Deadwood

BLACK
HILLS

Ft. Fetterman

The Stronghold

White River

Pine Ridge
Reservation
Wounded
Knee Creek
● Pine Ridge Agency

Rosebud
Reservation

Missouri River

SOUTH DAKOTA

Ft. Robinson
Harrison
Chadron
● Crawford
Red Cloud Agency No. 2

● Niobrara

Ft. Laramie
Red Cloud Agency No. 1

WYOMING

North Platte River

NEBRASKA

Omaha ●

━━━ Great Sioux Reservation
- - - Bozeman Trail

The West of Red Cloud

Introduction

How does one working within the Euro-American historical tradition write a biography of a nineteenth-century Native American? Given the vast cultural differences that exist – not to mention the long-standing historical conflict – is such a study as defined by Euro-American standards possible? What can be learned about a particular individual from the available sources? Biographers of noteworthy Native Americans have, for the most part, employed traditional methodologies in reconstructing these lives; few have looked to alternative documentation. One such alternative text is photography. Although it, like many sources, comes with a host of problems – the most important being that it was a visual medium invented and used exclusively during the nineteenth century by non-Natives – I contend that photography does provide the historian with unique insights into Native lives. Examining photographic portraits of the famous Oglala chief Red Cloud – Makhpiya-luta to his own people – suggests new ideas about his shifting status in American and Lakota society at the end of the nineteenth century and new possibilities for Native American biography.

Red Cloud provides a useful example because he posed before the camera on at least forty-five different occasions over a period of almost forty years. The total number of different photographs taken of Red Cloud is at least 128, making him the most photographed nineteenth-century Native American. I have highlighted 81 photographs that resulted from these sessions. (An appendix lists the 47 I have not reproduced.) Some of the most famous American photographers of this period worked with Red Cloud, including Mathew Brady, Alexander Gardner, Charles Bell, David Barry, Frank Rinehart, and Edward Curtis.

Though Red Cloud's interaction with photography was indeed special, it was not exceptional. Other nineteenth-century leaders – Geronimo, Chief Joseph, and Sarah Winnemucca, for example – were also photographed with great frequency. Nor was the practice of sitting for non-Native portraitists altogether new. Since the earliest period of Euro-American contact with Native Americans, both celebrated leaders and common tribespeople have agreed to pose for artists, often repeatedly. Photography's introduction in 1839 and subsequent popularization, however, coincided with a period of accelerated American expansionism in the trans-Mississippi West. As a result, the visual record of Native peoples dramatically increased during the second half of the nineteenth century.[1]

I want to acknowledge at the outset that transcultural photographic portraiture was never a neutral enterprise, as photographer and subject came together from distinctly different worlds to participate in what was many times a contested exchange. One could argue that all photographic portraiture is fraught with difficult ideological issues.[2] Given America's colonial legacy with the tribes of North America, however, unique cultural tensions were an additional burden in the interaction between Euro-American photographer and Native American subject. The dominant culture harbored strongly held, preconceived ideas about the "primitive" nature of Native peoples; tribal cultures looked at Euro-Americans as untrustworthy outsiders. Thus, mutual suspicion nearly always colored their interactions, especially when animosities already existed. Though Native Americans often agreed to cooperate, it is also true that many avoided the photographer's voyeuristic gaze altogether and also that non-Native photographers regularly created images without the permission of their subjects.[3] Because of its intrusive nature, photography was allowed no place at this time in many of the important rituals and ceremonies that were central to tribal cultures. Native resistance, though, only sporadically diminished the presence of these image-makers.[4]

The frequency with which commercial photographers sought out Native Americans for the purpose of procuring their portraits can be attributed to the great demand for such pictures within Euro-American society. As in the years before photography's invention, many people from a variety of backgrounds coveted images of Native American life. Both a fascination with disparate cultures and also a more basic desire among many white Americans to "play Indian" help explain the nineteenth-century urge to collect these photographs. Because of its

supposed transparency, photography gave viewers the ability to travel vicariously among foreign peoples, capturing the imagination of an eastern public that possessed only the most rudimentary and often distorted knowledge of Native American cultures.[5]

There were at least three different spaces for which these photographs were destined. For one, many portraits of Red Cloud were originally collected as interesting curiosities by members of a rapidly growing class of American consumers. Affixed to inexpensive cardboard backings, these *cartes de visite*, cabinet cards, stereographs, and, later, postcards served as popular keepsakes that could be archived in ornately decorated albums or displayed around the home. Collecting such images was both a source of entertainment and a marker of one's social and racial standing.[6] Second, photographic portraits of Native American subjects served a specific function in the expanding publishing industry. Given the medium's evidentiary nature, photographs often acted as the linchpin that attracted and held together a reader and a story. The competitiveness of the newspaper, magazine, and book businesses meant that editors were always seeking noteworthy photographs, even if these images were not always newsworthy. Third, there was a growing demand from the scientific community. In the burgeoning field of ethnology especially, American researchers looked to photography as a primary tool for investigating tribal cultures and analyzing their relationship with "the living races of mankind," to cite one leading study of this period.[7] Universities and new government agencies such as the Bureau of American Ethnology, founded in 1879, established substantial photographic archives that became the focus of scholarly research into Native American communities. In all these areas, in short, by the latter half of the nineteenth century, photography had pushed the image of the Native American before the American public to an unprecedented level of visibility.

The consequences of this visual revolution were profound. Photography not only caused consumers to see things they had never seen before; it also transformed their sense of identity, giving individuals a greater self-awareness of what they and others looked like. Because of the tendency to measure one's self against the photographed "other," many used these images to confirm existing ideas about a host of issues. Photography, growing at an exponential rate during the nineteenth century, also fueled a desire among the visually literate to know more about the world and their relationship to it. In the process, it altered society's thinking about its own history. As Euro-Americans worked to complete their subjugation and acculturation of the Native tribes of North America, photography influenced the manner in which that history unfolded, too.

In recent years, scholars have remarked that photography served as a tool, even a weapon, in the hands of nineteenth-century Euro-American colonizers.[8] Like other non-Native image-makers who intruded into traditional tribal cultures, photographers did help to legitimate the invasion and occupation of Native American lands. Creating images for mass circulation and consumption, they cast Native peoples into narrowly defined categories that assumed their eventual cultural extinction. The resulting photo-

graphs allowed non-Native viewers to project their own meanings onto these subjects, thereby simultaneously simplifying, abstracting, and romanticizing Native American culture. Though often held out as objective truth, these images displaced their subjects from an understandable context and inserted them into a new institutional setting, invariably distorting the public's perceptions of Native Americans. The portraits of Red Cloud and others therefore shed as much, often more, light on the dominant culture whose presence is invisible as on the Native subjects figured.

Photographs of Native Americans, though, were more than sources of evidence or entertainment in the service of Euro-American culture. Because a portrait is the result of a collaboration between at least two individuals, it is important to recognize the often overlooked role that Native American subjects themselves played in the ritual of portrait photography. Although many sessions were marked by awkward power imbalances, Native Americans were not rendered mute on such occasions. Many had their own reasons for entering into this exchange. They posed before the camera not as empty mannequins but rather as active participants in a larger transcultural dialogue. In effect, photography acted as what literary critic Mary Louise Pratt has called a "contact zone" in which disparate cultures interacted.[9] Though the nature of their cultural exchange would alter over time, this space provided participants with a new and unique meeting ground. Certain desirable subjects commanded a fee, but the majority of Native Americans used these sessions to further personal and political ends.

As in so many past encounters between Euro-Americans and indigenous peoples, however, the relationship between photographer and subject was not always a cooperative one; in fact, photographs frequently reveal the complex range of tensions and often competing aims that existed between different cultures. Nevertheless, many Native Americans such as Red Cloud continued to involve themselves in this exchange, an indication that they regarded photography as a vital medium through which to reconcile their differences. Though some scholars have argued that photography's introduction solidified existing power relations, the example of Red Cloud's use of photography complicates this idea.[10]

The nature of the interaction makes possible the idea that Native Americans could influence what transpired. During the nineteenth century there was rarely such a thing as a candid portrait. Photographic sessions were a highly formalized ritual that effectively made it impossible to create a spontaneous or "natural" image. A woodcut engraving (figure 1) from an 1881 issue of *Frank Leslie's Illustrated Newspaper*, picturing Charles Bell photographing a Brulé delegation in his Washington DC studio, gives an idea of how organized these sittings were. The bulky equipment photographers employed, the necessarily long exposures, the many onlookers, and the often elaborately designed studio settings all contributed to a rigidly defined structure. Nor were the sessions short; on several occasions, Red Cloud spent upward of two hours in the photographer's presence. Further, the fact that studio sessions usually preceded or followed some "official" public engagement gave them additional significance.

Even when Native Americans were photographed in places other than the studio, their interactions with photographers typically remained bounded by the same structure. Though Native Americans and non-Natives alike held special claim on certain places, photography created a unique set of circumstances that fluctuated only slightly with location. For Red Cloud and others, portrait photography served as a stage on which Native Americans and non-Natives continued to engage in a larger transcultural conversation.[11]

As photography tends to wrap individuals in a silent stillness and to remove them from time, Native Americans can be seen as the victims of a paralyzing Euro-American gaze. Scholars have noted that the genre of portrait photography has the effect of alienating its subjects, even depriving them of life; surrounded by the trappings of bourgeois culture, the carefully posed sitter becomes no more than a lifeless symbol.[12] The historic interaction between Red Cloud and the photographers who pictured him, however, runs counter to this claim. An active participant in the ritual of portrait photography, Red Cloud used these occasions to speak to both the dominant culture and his own people. The sociologist Roland Barthes has written that photography has a greater ability to resonate with viewers than do other visual mediums. Although one can only speculate as to why Red Cloud was drawn to photography, it was the case that photography's "punctum" – its capacity to grasp or "sting" a viewer psychologically – not only appealed to him but also presented him with a potentially powerful medium through which to communicate. Its reproducibility, ac-

1. "Washington, D. C. – Photographing an Indian delegation, in Bell's studio, for the government. – From a sketch by A. B. Shults." *Frank Leslie's Illustrated Newspaper*, September 10, 1881. Library of Congress, Washington DC (230270).

cessibility, and popularity also made photography additionally advantageous to this task.[13]

Thus, the photographic portraits of Red Cloud, beyond serving as a means of understanding Euro-Americans' perceptions of Native peoples, should also be read as semiautobiographical texts that reveal the various hopes and anxieties Red Cloud confronted during a transitional moment in Lakota history. Increasingly unable to live either apart from or within American society, Red Cloud and his people struggled to carve out an independent space for themselves during the second half of the nineteenth century. Fearful of being colonized by an outside force, Red Cloud used photography as a means of simultaneously paying deference to and resisting those Euro-Americans who sought to subjugate the Lakotas (of which the Oglalas were a subtribe). This process of "mimicry" allowed him to remain engaged in deliberations with government officials while at the same time offering him an opportunity to sabotage that authority. Between his first trip to the East in 1870 and his death in 1909, photography gave Red Cloud a tool with which to mark his presence and to negotiate relationships with others.[14]

Though mediated by the different photographers with whom he collaborated, his photographs reveal also an interest in self-fashioning. As political and social standing in Oglala society was determined more by public displays and performances than by hereditary association, the ability to manifest authority was vital. Red Cloud's embrace of photography to do this work was entirely new in the context of Native American society.[15] His willingness to appropriate an aspect of Euro-American culture for his own use was a creative yet potentially dangerous response to the predicament in which he found himself. Committed to ensuring both the Oglalas' political sovereignty and his own status as tribal leader, he looked beyond the risk of being objectified by the dominant culture and saw photography instead as an opportunity to further the dialogue between the two nations. As historian Nell Painter has demonstrated in her biography of Sojourner Truth, the illiterate former slave and famed nineteenth-century abolitionist, photography was a means whereby marginalized individuals could shape their public identity.[16] Like Sojourner Truth, Red Cloud asserted his presence through the ceremony of portrait photography. Refusing to allow others within Euro-American society to define him, he seized upon this new technology for his work of self-representation – as, indeed, did thousands of Americans who invested the currency of photography with various hopes and dreams during the nineteenth century.

Within Lakota society the means of establishing a public self have been forever evolving. In addition to storytelling, which continues to serve as the principal vehicle for self-fashioning, pictographs have traditionally been a visual mode that individuals employed to mark their presence. Drawings on animal hides and rock walls served as a key precedent in the development of new visual texts, including, most importantly in the nineteenth century, ledger-book art. Though introduced by Euro-Americans, ledger books became significant to Native peoples as places where they could record their own history. Red Cloud's involvement with photography parallels their introduction in many respects. Both aspects of visual culture emerged during the same period; both were initially brought to tribal communities in attempts by non-Natives to study Native Americans; and Native peoples learned to use both mediums for their own purposes. Like ledger drawings, photography became a place where the Lakotas had an opportunity to contest the histories being established about them and the policies being enacted "for their benefit."[17]

Red Cloud's interest in making himself visible was an important choice in a larger struggle for cultural survival. As Euro-Americans aimed to render Native Americans invisible through a program of forced acculturation, he demanded that others see him, preferably on his own terms, though that was often not possible. Still, given the difficult circumstances in which the Oglalas found themselves at the end of the nineteenth century, it was a risk that Red Cloud felt was worth taking. Other Oglala leaders felt differently. The famed warrior Crazy Horse, for example, never posed for a photographer, a decision indicative of his unyielding commitment to a campaign of warfare against the United States. Though a great military leader himself in the years prior to the 1868 Fort Laramie treaty, which led to the establishment of the Great Sioux Reservation, Red Cloud favored dialogue rather than hostilities with the Americans. His embrace of photography was consistent with this new outlook.

That Red Cloud took seriously his role as a representative of his people was especially evident in the photographic studio. Repeated comments by photographers with whom he interacted suggest that he approached these sessions with a great deliberateness. For example, William Henry Jackson reported in his 1877 catalogue of Native American photographs that "while Spotted Tail [had] a lively vein of humor in his character, and loved to indulge in a little joke, Red Cloud [was] all dignity and seriousness" before the camera.[18] And even though he posed for his portrait on more occasions than any other nineteenth-century Native American, he did sometimes refuse to participate, an indication that he played an active part in shaping his self-representation. The fact that no one ever photographed Red Cloud surreptitiously – a common practice among many photographers of Native peoples – further testifies to his ability to manage these proceedings.

Though he sometimes accepted money and other gifts in exchange for posing before the camera, he regarded photography principally as a mediating tool. When deliberating about some issue, Red Cloud displayed a tendency throughout his political life to formalize all exchanges with others. Often this meant finding someone or something to serve as a go-between. As Nebraska writer Mari Sandoz once explained, Red Cloud was "putting always a third person between them and himself." Taken from an account that her father provided of his encounter with the Oglala chief in the summer of 1886, this brief description suggests Red Cloud's characteristic desire to speak through a mediating structure.[19] Because he spoke no English, Red Cloud always traveled with an interpreter, an obvious go-between, and it is noteworthy that his interpreter was often photographed by his side. Likewise, the medium of photography itself allowed him to shape the manner in which he presented himself and his ideas. Furthermore, it gave him the ability to preserve a certain distance between himself and Euro-American culture. As postcolonial theorist Homi Bhabha has explained, at the heart of mimicry is the idea of maintaining one's sense of autonomy and control.[20]

Others who knew him also stressed his unique ability to balance the demands of two disparate cultures. James Mooney, an influential anthropologist at the Bureau of American Ethnology who interacted with Red Cloud on numerous occasions, concluded insightfully that he "was a warrior and a diplomat, and knew how to be an Indian while keeping in favor with the government."[21] No Lakota leader of his era was better able to achieve and maintain this delicate balance. Pine Ridge agent John R. Brennan reached a similar conclusion in summing up the chief's legacy: "Red Cloud, like Sitting Bull, was fighting for a principle, but was trying to accomplish his ends in a different way. He was working for what he considered the best interests of his people and evidently thought he could accomplish

2. Red Cloud's bedroom, Pine Ridge Agency, South Dakota, 1891. Photograph by Clarence G. Morledge. Nebraska State Historical Society, Lincoln (RG2845:119-9).

3. Home of Red Cloud at Pine Ridge Agency, 1891. Photograph by Clarence G. Morledge. National Anthropological Archives, Smithsonian Institution, Washington DC (52541).

more by working inside the breastworks than outside and on the warpath."[22] In a sense, then, the photographer's studio became one of Red Cloud's most important battlegrounds. A skillful politician, he used rituals such as photography to campaign on behalf of both himself and his people.

It is also revealing that Red Cloud actively collected photographs himself. Clarence G. Morledge's 1891 picture of the interior of Red Cloud's home at Pine Ridge (figure 2) shows some of those that he hung on his bedroom wall. Included in his collection was an earlier group portrait that Morledge had taken of Red Cloud and his wife, Pretty Owl, plus an unidentified third person, outside the front door of his two-story home (figure 3). The presence of these photographs and his use of them as mementos suggest the extent to which he came to embrace aspects of Euro-American society. Furthermore, his willingness to allow Morledge to photograph the interior of his home on this and one other occasion points to the accommodating relationship he shared with the young photographer. Also pictured in this view, Red Cloud's collection of American flags and his portraits of the Virgin Mary and of Jesus Christ wearing a crown of thorns further indicate that he could maintain commitments to a variety of often conflicting beliefs. Red Cloud seems to be suggesting much about both his allegiance to those traditions and the strength of his own authority. To him, this photograph served as an icon of power as much as did these American and Christian symbols.

The items that Red Cloud collected and displayed in his bedroom were often gifts presented to him on special occasions, but he also actively sought out photographs and other mementos. In an 1882 letter to Commissioner of Indian Affairs Hiram Price he revealed his enthusiasm for collecting photographs of family and friends. Sent not long after Red Cloud returned from his sixth trip to Washington, the letter asked Price to send a photograph of two Indian Bureau employees he had befriended there: "I would say that the two men referred to whose pictures I want are Mr. Stamca in the Secretary's office and the one with the black hair and goatee or small whiskers who occupied a desk near yours. I shall be very glad to get their pictures as they are friends of mine."[23] Though the ritual of transcultural photographic portraiture is often seen as dehumanizing, it is evident that Red Cloud invested it with significance.

Still, can one know Red Cloud through photographs of him? Despite the fact that he played an active role in the construction of these images, the promise of knowing an individual through a visual text is always deceptive. Historian Graham Clarke has written that photographs conceal as much as they reveal: "As the formal representation of a face or body, [a portrait photograph] is, by its very nature, enigmatic. And part of this enigma is embedded in the nature of identity as itself ambiguous, for the portrait advertises an individual who endlessly eludes the single, static and fixed frame of a public portrait. In this sense, the very terms of the portrait photograph's status are problematic."[24] While they may seem transparent to viewers' eyes, photographs are never mirror images, as appearances always fail to illuminate entirely. Instead, photographs are fragments like pottery shards that can tell only part of the story.

Chief Red Cloud's Bed Room

Home of Chief Red Cloud at Pine Ridge Agency

Total recall is not possible, especially when photographer and subject do not share common aims or cultural heritages.[25] Poet Walt Whitman reached a similar conclusion in an 1884 essay reminiscing about his onetime employment at the Bureau of Indian Affairs.

My here-alluded-to experience in the Indian Bureau produced one very definite conclusion, as follows: There is something about these aboriginal Americans, in their highest characteristic representations, essential traits, and the ensemble of their physique and physiognomy – something very remote, very lofty, arousing comparisons with our own civilized ideals – something that our literature, portrait painting, etc., have never caught, and that will almost certainly never be transmitted to the future, even as a reminiscence. No biographer, no historian, no artist, has grasp'd it – perhaps could not grasp it. It is so different, so far outside our standards of eminent humanity.[26]

This dual predicament – the limitations of texts in conveying meaning and outsiders' inability to appreciate fully and to describe exactly a culture different from their own – is a constant challenge for historians, whether they are working with written or with visual materials. Though a single photograph, like a single written document, will never do justice to the complexities of a subject, a series of images provides an opportunity to note similarities and contradictions over a period of time and thus may lead to a fuller understanding. When viewed together, the photographic portraits of Red Cloud allow one to compare how he positioned himself over time before the camera and, by extension, before both the American public and his fellow Oglalas.

No records exist that reveal what Red Cloud thought of his appearance. Given the frequency with which he visited photographers' studios, though, he must have had a good idea of it. He also knew how others looked in photographic portraits, and surely he modified his own appearance in response. By analyzing, for example, the outfits that he wore, the poses that he struck, and the individuals with whom he was photographed, the contemporary scholar can gain new insight into Red Cloud's engagement with both Euro-American and Lakota society during specific periods of his life. Because a non-Native photographer was always responsible for "taking" these portraits and because their number is limited, significant gaps and inconsistencies in this autobiographical record certainly remain. It is important to remember that there is much that photography cannot see.[27]

It is also important in evaluating these photographs to identify the particular type. Not all of Red Cloud's portraits belong to the same genre. Some are half length, others full. Although most are direct frontal views, a few are in profile. Some are taken outdoors, but more are in a photographer's studio or some other building. Many include only Red Cloud, but there are plenty that feature him among groups of various sizes. Given this diversity, one must consider the exact nature of each photograph to understand more fully both the photographer's particular investment in creating such a view and also Red Cloud's appropriation of the photographic moment. Indeed, different situations meant different things to photographer and subject, and it was not uncommon for competing visions to exist.[28] Because photography figures only a part of a particular moment or scene, investigating those who were present though not pictured – not to mention activities that occurred outside the photograph's frame – provides further opportunities to evaluate this cultural exchange.

Most important, to unlock knowledge from these texts, one must also situate this series of portraits within the historical context of both Euro-American and Lakota society in the late nineteenth century. In the past, photographs of Native American subjects were predominantly framed by non-Natives with an interest in maintaining centuries-old stereotypes. Viewing this series through the lens of Oglala society, however, provides a much different perspective. When one considers his portraits in this light, Red Cloud no longer represents the "vanishing American" or the "exotic savage." Instead, one sees him as an aging leader fighting to preserve his tribe's political sovereignty and to maintain his own status as a leader of the Oglala people. Early biographies of Red Cloud, choosing to focus on his often celebrated military prowess, consistently paid less attention to his role as a tribal diplomat.[29] The introduction of these photographic portraits is intended to return attention to this important aspect of his career.

Red Cloud was forty-nine years old when he first encountered the visual medium of photography in the spring of 1870; consequently, this book concentrates principally on the second half of his life, an era in which historian Catherine Price has shown that the "United States, through its agents, superintendents, and commissioners endeavored to reshape Lakota society in accordance with American ideals."[30] For an understanding of the decisions he made

during this period, though, it is important first to note something about his upbringing and rise to power. If the latter half of his life was taken up by a series of diplomatic conflicts, the first half was characterized by numerous contests both on the battlefield and in tribal politics.

Red Cloud was born in the spring of 1821 along Blue Water Creek, a tributary of the North Platte in western Nebraska. He lost his father to alcoholism when he was only a small child; thereafter, he was raised by his mother's brother, a chief of the Bad Face band named Smoke. Like most Oglala boys, Red Cloud grew up eager to become part of the warrior culture that dominated male society. At the age of sixteen he participated in his first war party and returned home with a Pawnee scalp. His bravery and success as a warrior over the next three decades helped to propel him into increasingly important positions within his tribe.[31] By the early 1860s he had become recognized by his own people as one of the Oglalas' principal war leaders.

In the years after the American Civil War, Red Cloud's name became familiar throughout the United States and its territories. This national notoriety was a direct result of increased tensions between the two cultures. Upset by the growing number of non-Native settlers who were crossing Lakota territory, Red Cloud helped to orchestrate a military and diplomatic resistance to American authorities. Forts that the U.S. Army had recently constructed in Wyoming to protect the Bozeman Trail (which cut through Native lands to reach the goldfields to the west) were the targets of numerous raids, and a series of government-sponsored peace initiatives were spurned. Of special note to this project, during the summer of 1866, Ridgeway Glover, a young photographer from Philadelphia, was killed while taking pictures for *Frank Leslie's Illustrated Newspaper* near Fort Philip Kearny along the Bozeman Trail. A soldier's letter to *Leslie's* related the gruesome details of his death: "He was out sketching for you – his long absence occasioned no little anxiety – and a party went out (members of the 18th Infantry), and found his body. The head was found a few yards off, completely severed from the trunk, scalped. The body was disemboweled, and then fire placed in the cavity. His remains, horribly mutilated, were decently interred, and a search was made for his apparatus, but could not be found. Mr. Glover, though an eccentric and peculiar being, was generally respected by all who knew him." [32] Although it would be misleading to conclude that Red Cloud and others feared photography, Glover's death does attest to the tense situation that existed on the northern Plains at this time and also to the fact that photographers were not immune to such hostilities.

Most significant in cementing the American public's perception of Red Cloud as the epitome of Lakota aggressiveness and might was his leadership in what became popularly known as the Fetterman Massacre. Having been drawn away from the protection that Fort Philip Kearny provided, Colonel William J. Fetterman and eighty-two soldiers were attacked and killed in a rout by Red Cloud's forces on December 21, 1866. Though no American soldiers survived to relate the details of the battle, a woodcut engraving from *Harper's Weekly* (figure 4) purported to depict this event. Such images, together with newspaper accounts

claiming to provide readers with a sketch of the "massacre," contributed greatly to Red Cloud's inclusion among the great enemies of the nation.

Throughout the next year, Red Cloud continued to wage war on the U.S. Army. In July, President Andrew Johnson created the Indian Peace Commission to restart negotiations with the Lakotas, but they quickly stalled when the Oglalas refused to participate. In the popular literature of the day, this ongoing conflict became known as Red Cloud's War. In fact, Americans perceived Red Cloud to be the triumphant leader of the entire Lakota nation, a designation that misconstrued his actual position and Lakota systems of political authority. At that time, Oglala tribesmen recognized Red Cloud as a *blotahunka*, or war party leader, but it would be several more years before his people designated him an *itancan*, or chief, the leader who sat at the head of the tribal council. [33]

The year 1868 brought renewed efforts at quelling hostilities on the northern Plains. Peace talks were again initiated, and U.S. authorities sent high-ranking officials to meet Lakota leaders at Fort Laramie. Though several delegates agreed to discuss the situation, Red Cloud again refused, stating that he would not sign a peace treaty until the American military abandoned every fort along the Bozeman Trail. Only when this and other concessions were agreed upon later in the fall did the Oglalas reluctantly suspend their military campaign. The ensuing treaty ended the war and established the Great Sioux Reservation.

Although the Fort Laramie treaty of 1868 gave the Lakotas control over a specifically defined area within the Dakota Territory, it also paved the way for the in-

4. "The Indian battle and massacre near Fort Philip Kearney, Dacotah Territory, December 21, 1866." *Harper's Weekly*, March 23, 1867. Library of Congress, Washington DC.

troduction of a host of new non-Native figures – Christian missionaries, teachers, and government agents – whose increasing presence on the reservation would dramatically reshape the cultural landscape in the coming years. The completion of the transcontinental railroad in the summer of 1869 also accelerated the number of settlers moving onto and across the Plains. These newcomers would further challenge the Oglalas' ability to maintain their tribal autonomy.[34]

Red Cloud made his first trip to the East, accompanied by twenty other Oglalas, in June 1870. Commissioner of Indian Affairs Ely S. Parker and Secretary of the Interior Jacob D. Cox had invited the delegation to Washington to negotiate a treaty that would allow the building of roads through the Black Hills and the Big Horn Mountains. Government officials also invited a delegation of Brulés, led by Spotted Tail, to participate in these discussions. Though both groups were in Washington at the same time, they tended to remain apart because of their leaders' dispute over the recent killing of Big Mouth, a close friend of Red Cloud.

During his meeting with President Ulysses S. Grant and other government officials, Red Cloud, whom Oglala counselors had selected to serve as his tribe's primary spokesman, denounced the new road initiative and spelled out a variety of complaints about American violations of the treaty that Lakota leaders had signed two years earlier, the recent construction of Fort Fetterman along the Bozeman

Trail being foremost on this list. Grant, however, was unmoved by Red Cloud's criticism. Stating his hope that the military stationed in the West would work together with the Lakotas to ensure peaceful relations, the president refused to act on this and other demands. Red Cloud left Washington disappointed about the lack of progress on these issues.

Before returning to the West, however, the delegation traveled to New York City, where Red Cloud spoke before a capacity audience at the Cooper Institute. A woodcut engraving from *Frank Leslie's Illustrated Newspaper* provides one artist's rendering of that occasion (figure 5). Through an interpreter, Red Cloud continued his effort at educating American authorities about his tribe's situation, concluding,

I have tried to get from my Great Father what is right and just. I have not altogether succeeded. I want you to believe with me, to know with me, that which is right and just. I represent the whole Sioux nation. They will be grieved by what I represent. I am no Spotted Tail, who will say one thing one day and be bought for a fish the next. Look at me! I am poor, naked, but I am chief of a nation. We do not ask for riches; we do not want much, but we want our children properly trained, brought up. We look to you for that. Riches here do no good. We can not take them away with us out of this world, but we want to have love and peace. The money, the riches that we have in this world, as Secretary Cox lately told me, we can not take these into the next world. If this is so, I would like to know why the commissioners who are sent out there do nothing but rob to get the riches of this world away from us. I was brought up among traders and those who came out there in the early times. I had good times

with them; they treated me mostly always right, always well. They taught me to use clothes, to use tobacco, to use firearms and ammunition. This was all very well until the Great Father sent another kind of man out there – men who drank whiskey, men who were so bad that the Great Father could not keep them at home, so he sent them out there. I have sent a great many words to the Great Father, but they never reached him. They were drowned on the way, and I was afraid the words I spoke lately to the Great Father would not reach you, so I came to speak to you myself; and now I am going away to my home. I want to have men sent out to my people whom we know and can trust. I am glad I have come here. You belong in the East, and I belong in the West, and I am glad that I have come here, and that we understand one another. I am very much obliged to you for listening to me. I go home this afternoon. I hope you will think of what I have said to you. I bid you all an affectionate farewell.[35]

Following the speech, Commissioner Parker invited Red Cloud and the rest of his party to Mathew Brady's photographic studio on Broadway. This was not the first such invitation the delegation had received. Red Cloud had already declined to sit before Brady's camera back in Washington, and he again explained that "it did not suit him to do so. When asked why, he said he was not a white man, but a Sioux, and that he was not dressed for the occasion." The journalist reporting this event for *Frank Leslie's Illustrated Newspaper* also suggested that Red Cloud and others were afraid the "Great Spirit would be angry with them, and they would die. . . . Despairing of convincing Red Cloud and Spotted Tail of the improbability of the Great Spirit being an-

5. "New York City. – The Sioux chief, Red Cloud, in the Great Hall of the Cooper Institute, surrounded by the Indian delegation of braves and squaws, addressing a New York audience on the wrongs done to his people. – From a sketch by our special artist." *Frank Leslie's Illustrated Newspaper,* July 2, 1870. Library of Congress, Washington DC.

gry with them for having their pictures taken, Mr. Brady permitted them to go back to their native wilderness as they had left it – unphotographed."[36]

The two declined invitations represented Red Cloud's first encounter with photography, and his refusals suggest his hesitancy to be involved in what he initially regarded as an exclusively Euro-American ritual. His unwillingness to participate may also have stemmed from his frustration over stalled negotiations with government officials. Here, as in

subsequent years, Red Cloud considered photography an extension of a larger transcultural dialogue which, though he balked at this first opportunity, he would come to welcome in the future. At the same time, it is important to see the journalist's follow-up comment about "the Great Spirit being angry with them" as characteristic of the dominant culture's inclination to perpetuate colorful stereotypes of Native peoples. Such was the risk of entering into this type of cultural exchange. The fact that Red Cloud would later participate so often reveals his overriding interest in serving as a mediator between the Oglalas and the United States.

Red Cloud's decision to face the camera as often as he did was also motivated by his personal desire to show not only the American public and his fellow tribespeople but also himself that he remained a vital presence within Oglala society. In the years that followed his first interaction with photography, Red Cloud faced numerous challenges from both inside and outside his tribe. Though he was a much respected leader, the second half of his life was difficult. Intratribal feuding and the increased Euro-American presence on the northern Plains threatened repeatedly to upset any semblance of stability that followed the signing of the Fort Laramie treaty in 1868. American authorities pressed him and his tribe to cede protected lands and to adopt Euro-American ways; at the same time, young Lakota leaders questioned his commitment to political sovereignty and his ability to lead. It is noteworthy that in the series of autobiographical statements he gave to his non-Native friend Sam Deon in 1893, Red Cloud wanted to speak only about that period in his life before the escalation of diplomatic tensions with the Americans.[37] The attention that photography accorded him helped to support the notion that he remained an important leader during the second half of his life, though many of these photographs, especially in his old age, reveal his fragile situation.[38]

The studios and other locales where Red Cloud posed for the camera were the sites of a complex dance between him and the Euro-Americans who gathered there. Since each side had its own motivations for coming together, these photographs are ultimately the result of an often awkward, always politically charged collaboration. Though Euro-Americans used photography in an attempt to separate and subjugate Native Americans, Red Cloud embraced photographic portraits as an alternative means of voicing personal and tribal concerns. They helped to reaffirm his physical presence in a world that wanted to render him and his people invisible. By examining the transformations that occurred over time in his confrontation with the white man's camera, one can chart not simply the way in which American society manipulated and appropriated an important chief's image but also the manner in which he attempted to negotiate his increasingly marginalized status. In a sense, the photographs in this volume serve as the second half of his autobiography, the half that he refused to divulge to Deon.

1. First Exposure, 1870–1877

Having battled American incursions against the Lakotas for many years from his home on the northern Plains, Red Cloud moved his campaign of resistance after 1870 to the negotiating table – and the photographer's studio. The increase of Euro-American settlers and the concurrent decline in the region's natural resources account in part for this shift. Hoping to play an active role in the implementation of the new agency system agreed upon in the 1868 Fort Laramie treaty, Red Cloud traveled often to the East. Between 1870 and 1877 he led four different Oglala delegations to Washington DC to meet with government representatives. Although he avoided Mathew Brady's camera on his first visit, in 1870, he soon saw photography as an opportunity to build relationships and to attract attention to himself and his people. Given the marketability of his name, Euro-Americans eagerly pursued photographic images of the Oglala leader for their own purposes.

Studio of Mathew Brady, Washington DC, May 28, 1872

Red Cloud visited Washington for two weeks in the spring of 1872. Upset about several ongoing problems at the Oglalas' newly designated agency on the North Platte River – known officially as the Red Cloud Agency – he and twenty-six followers, plus agent James W. Daniels, came to Washington to meet again with President Grant. Red Cloud wanted to talk to officials about the increasing number of encroachments by Euro-American settlers onto Lakota lands. Furthermore, he hoped that government authorities would supply them with more goods, including guns and ammunition for hunting game.

For his part, Grant was eager to discuss with Red Cloud the circumstances behind the recent robbery and murder of a rancher near the reservation. His larger goal, though, was to initiate a conversation about the possibility of removing the Lakotas to the so-called Indian Territory (present-day Oklahoma). Grant's proposal would have allowed for the expansion of Euro-American settlement on the northern Plains and furthered the government's long-standing vision of segregating Native tribes within a single, concentrated area on the southern Plains.

On the morning of May 28, Red Cloud led a group of other Oglala leaders – "in full war costume," according to one newspaper report – to the White House for their appointment with President Grant. After welcoming them, Grant proceeded to articulate his hopes for the Oglalas and his desire to assist them in their quest "to become self-supporting":

The time must come when, with the great growth of population here, the game will be gone, and your people will then have to resort

6. Red Cloud, 1872. Photograph by Mathew Brady. National Anthropological Archives, Smithsonian Institution, Washington DC (53551).

to other means of support; and while there is time we would like to teach you new modes of living that will secure you in the future and be a safe means of livelihood. I want to see the Indians get upon land where they can look forward to permanent homes for themselves and their children. . . . If, at any time, you feel like moving to what is known as the Cherokee country, which is a large territory, with an admirable climate where you would never suffer from the cold and where you could have lands set apart to remain exclusively your own, we would set apart a large tract of land that would belong to you and your children.[1]

Red Cloud chose not to respond to this idea. Already angry that government authorities had moved the Oglalas' agency across the North Platte without warning while he had recently been away, he sought Grant's support for relocating the agency farther north to a new location on the White River. The proposal intrigued federal officials because it would move the Oglalas farther from the tracks of the Union Pacific Railroad, and since Euro-American settlement was concentrated along the railroad line, homesteaders were agitating to keep Native communities far removed. By summer's end the government had approved this plan.

Before their appointment at the White House, Red Cloud and several other members of the delegation visited Mathew Brady's studio on Pennsylvania Avenue – long a traditional custom for out-of-town dignitaries. Though he had refused Brady's offer to photograph him two years earlier, Red Cloud submitted on this occasion – perhaps as a gesture expressing his desire to work with American authorities in reaching some diplomatic understanding.

Seated in a chair that Brady reserved for presidents, senators, and other high-ranking officials, Red Cloud adopts a statesmanlike pose (figure 6). For more than twenty years, Brady had been collecting photographs of "illustrious Americans" for display in his New York and Washington galleries. Since no photographer had ever made Red Cloud's portrait before, Brady must have been excited to add this image to his so-called National Portrait Collection.

Studio of Alexander Gardner, Washington DC, May 30, 1872

The Oglala delegation remained in the nation's capital for two weeks visiting with various government officials and other interested parties. Most Native American delegations to Washington were summoned there, but Red Cloud had initiated this trip himself. As he explained through an interpreter before heading east, "I want to take some of my people and show them the White Man's ways. I want to be better acquainted with [President Grant] and have a talk about many things. I want to tell him what I have done since I saw him."[2]

Though the delegation had a number of scheduled meetings, they also enjoyed a fair amount of free time. Indian Bureau officials led them on tours of prominent Washington institutions, and many, including Red Cloud, made appointments for medical checkups with local doctors. Two days after visiting Mathew Brady's studio, they also spent a lengthy morning in the gallery of Alexander Gardner. A onetime assistant to Brady, Gardner now ran his own commercial studio in Washington and hosted many tribal delegations there. Thanks to his photographic reportage of both the Civil War and the government's well-publicized peace talks with the Lakotas at Fort Laramie in 1868, Gardner enjoyed a national reputation.[3] On this occasion he photographed sixteen members of the Oglala delegation.

Not surprisingly, given his public stature, Red Cloud received special attention, and Gardner completed at least four images of him. In the first view (figure 7), Red Cloud's hair is braided and he wears a single feather, indicative of his rank as a chief. He has wrapped a blanket around his waist, wears moccasins, and holds a beaded pipe bag. Behind him Gardner has placed a photographic brace, the base of which is partially visible. Common equipment in photographic studios of this time, braces helped to keep a subject's head and body still during the length of the exposure.

Though officials from the Indian Bureau usually arranged photographic sessions for tribal delegations, the individual responsible for Red Cloud's visit to Gardner's studio was William Blackmore, a wealthy Englishman with interests in both land speculation in the American West and the welfare of Native tribes. Having first become interested in Native Americans on seeing the painter George Catlin's extensive archive of painted portraits and ethnographic material in London, Blackmore wanted to assemble his own collection for exhibit in a museum he was building in Salisbury, England.

He began collecting photographs in 1863. When the Smithsonian lost its archive of Native American portraits in a fire two years later, he approached their officials, hoping they would help finance

7. Red Cloud, 1872. Photograph by Alexander Gardner. Amon Carter Museum, Fort Worth TX (P1967.1784).

8. Red Cloud with William Blackmore, 1872. Photograph by
Alexander Gardner. Yale Collection of Western Americana,
Beinecke Rare Book and Manuscript Library, New Haven CT.

his project in exchange for duplicates of
the resulting pictures. Like many at the
time, Blackmore believed that Native
American communities were rapidly vanishing, and collecting photographs was
his way of preserving a scientific record of
the culture for posterity. Though Smithsonian officials initially refused to allo-
cate money for this purpose, in 1872 they
did establish a relationship with Blackmore to assist his project.[4]

Of the more than two thousand photographs that Blackmore commissioned,
the Englishman himself appears only in
the portrait shown in figure 8. Standing
at Red Cloud's side, he looks down and
shakes hands with the famous chief, who
is seated on a studio chair and does not
return Blackmore's gaze. Red Cloud continues to wear a blanket around his waist
but has now put on a dark jacket. As
Blackmore wears a jacket too, perhaps
Red Cloud wanted to dress more like his
host. (One reason he had balked at being
photographed two years earlier was that
he did not feel he was properly dressed.)[5]
In addition, Red Cloud has removed his
feather and unbraided his hair, allowing
it to fall freely over his shoulders. Such
adjustments indicate that these sessions
featured often complicated interactions
between participants and that Red Cloud
was cognizant of his public appearance.

Most revealing, though, is the fact that
the two men are shaking hands, suggesting mutual respect. Although the nature
of their relationship is uncertain, this
photograph seems to indicate that they
formed a friendship during their time together in Washington. Warren K.
Moorehead, an anthropologist who befriended Red Cloud in the 1890s, corrobo-
rated this idea in a later historical study.

Having noted that Red Cloud had initially been reluctant to sit before the
white man's camera, Moorehead explained that he agreed to pose for Blackmore "because he knew that the British
treated the Indians well, and that for a
century Indians in Canada lived unmo-
lested, whereas over the American border,
bloodshed and robbery were rampant."[6]

As a young man growing up near Fort
Laramie, Red Cloud had interacted frequently with Euro-American soldiers and
traders. His remark in his speech at the
Cooper Institute in 1870, that he often
formed positive relationships with persons from outside the tribal community,
seems to be confirmed by this occasion in
Gardner's studio. Red Cloud could work
with individuals such as Blackmore.

Blackmore spent more than two weeks
in Washington before leaving with Ferdinand Hayden's expedition to the newly
designated Yellowstone National Park.
During this time he was often in the
company of Red Cloud and the other
Oglalas, visiting many of Washington's
landmark sites. On the day after Red
Cloud's meeting with President Grant,
Blackmore chartered a steamer to take the
delegation on an excursion down the
Potomac River. Sidford Hamp, Blackmore's seventeen-year-old nephew, described their picnic lunch:

It was such a lark to see the Indians eat. One
mixed strawberries and olives together, another
plum cake and pickled oysters. Some ate holding the things in their hands and some ate ice
cream, pineapple and fowl all at once with
knife and fork. Together they managed very
well. During desert Uncle made a speech and
proposed health to the President, the Queen,
and the Chiefs, and their squaws, &c. The Indi-

9. Red Cloud, 1872. Photograph by Alexander Gardner. National Anthropological Archives, Smithsonian Institution, Washington DC (3235).

ans answered but I could not hear the interpreter. Afterwards "Red Cloud" made a very good speech and said that "he and the others were very much pleased with their treat, and that he should tell his people at home."[7]

It was on the following day that Blackmore led the Oglala delegation to Gardner's studio. Though this visit was in one sense an extension of their diplomatic activities together, it was also an occasion to further Blackmore's ethnographic study. That goal is apparent in one particular photograph, a close-up, direct frontal portrait of Red Cloud from the waist up (figure 9). As opposed to the earlier two Gardner images, here Red Cloud peers straight ahead toward the camera. His hands hold up the blanket he carries so that the design on its ornamental beaded strip is readily visible.

Although it is not known who orchestrated this awkward pose, given Blackmore's intended use for this collection, it is likely that Gardner asked Red Cloud to adopt it. The catalogue of Blackmore's collection of Native American photographs compiled by William Henry Jackson in 1877 supports the idea that Red Cloud has been made into a kind of specimen. In listing this photograph, Jackson wrote about both Red Cloud's history and his physical build: "He is now about 45 years of age, six feet in height, and straight as an arrow; his face, which is of a dark red, is indicative of indomitable courage and firmness, and his full, piercing eyes seem to take in at a glance the character of friend or foe."[8] The incorporation of this image into an ethnographic discourse suggests the contested nature of the exchanges that took place before the camera. Though both Red Cloud and

10. *Standing, left to right:* Julius Meyer, Red Cloud; *seated:* Sitting Bull (Oglala), Swift Bear, Spotted Tail, 1875. Photograph by Frank Currier. National Anthropological Archives, Smithsonian Institution, Washington DC (3684-D)

Blackmore saw photography as an important tool, each had his own reasons for coming together at the photog-rapher's studio.

Studio of Frank Currier, Omaha, Nebraska, May 1875

Red Cloud made his third trip to Washington in the spring of 1875 (government authorities having denied his request the previous fall). He traveled east to express his growing concern regarding several subjects: he was upset at the conduct of John J. Saville, the new head of the Red Cloud Agency; he was troubled by the recent gold-hunting expedition into the Black Hills led by George A. Custer; and he was angry about a new government effort to move the Lakota reservation to the Indian Territory. For their part, though possible removal remained an important issue, American officials had another reason for wanting to meet with tribal leaders: namely, they wanted to purchase the mineral-rich Black Hills from the Lakotas.

On their way east the delegation stopped in Omaha, Nebraska, where a local clothing store presented Red Cloud with a new suit. The *Omaha Republican* reported that he immediately changed into this outfit, thereby provoking his companions' jealousy.[9] The photograph in figure 10 was probably taken not long afterward in Frank Currier's studio on Farnham Street. Before an elaborately painted backdrop, Red Cloud, wearing his new suit and holding the same blanket as in Gardner's studio three years earlier, stands beside the interpreter Julius Meyer, who wears a tasseled and beaded leather shirt. The other three delegation leaders – from left to right, Sitting Bull (an Oglala, not the more famous Hunkpapa leader) and the Brulé chiefs Swift Bear and Spotted Tail – are seated in front.

Meyer acted as their host in Omaha and was the person responsible for taking them to Currier's studio. In addition to serving as an interpreter, Meyer also ran a store on Farnham Street known as the Indian Wigwam, where he sold various objects created by tribal artists. Having spent several years living with the Lakotas, he was regarded as an expert on the region and its Native peoples.[10] Nevertheless, the delegation demanded to be paid for participating in this photographic session. Meyer ended up covering all their expenses in Omaha and giving these four leaders two ponies each.[11] Such was the price that Red Cloud and other Native leaders often expected for their cooperation.

Red Cloud's involvement also reveals much about the status of his various relationships. In this case, his willingness to pose with Spotted Tail suggests that their feud was less heated than it once had been; five years earlier, while each was visiting Washington for the first time, the two leaders had refused to meet. Though now on friendlier terms, they remained rivals during the 1870s, each vying to be recognized by government authorities as the premier spokeperson for the Lakotas. Small wonder that the presentation of this suit from a local clothing store pleased Red Cloud: it indicated his special standing outside the reservation, and he was not shy about wearing it to Currier's studio.

In a second Currier photograph, Red Cloud is seated at the right in the front row (figure 11). Two other interpreters, Louis Bordeaux and William Garnett,

have joined Meyer behind the four Lakota leaders. Meyer is not wearing his decorated leather shirt in this pose. Whereas the previous group portrait served principally as a publicity photograph for Meyer's use, this image functioned as the more official delegation portrait. Interestingly, the government agents who accompanied the group do not appear. Although their absence from this and other group photographs seems to suggest that these sessions were not politically significant, visits to photographers' studios – like the trips of which they were a part – were in fact always highly charged diplomatic maneuvers: agents lavished attention on the Native leaders, all the while procuring images that could serve a variety of purposes. Leaders such as Red Cloud, in turn, entered into such exchanges believing that their cooperation would serve them well in future negotiations.

In Washington the delegation met again with President Grant and Commissioner of Indian Affairs Edward P. Smith. As on the two previous trips, though, little was accomplished: Red Cloud's complaints failed to move Grant and Smith, and the government's proposal to buy the Black Hills at first only offended the Lakota leaders. When the delegation did finally agree to discuss it, they demanded financial support from the government for seven generations. Red Cloud explained, "Maybe you white people think that I ask too much from the government, but I think those hills extend clear to the sky–maybe they go above the sky, and that is the reason I ask for so much. I think that the Black Hills are worth more than all the wild beasts and all the tame beasts in the possession

11. *Standing, left to right:* Louis Bordeaux, William Garnett, Julius Meyer; *seated, left to right:* Sitting Bull (Oglala), Swift Bear, Spotted Tail, Red Cloud, 1875. Photograph by Frank Currier. Original unlocated; reprint, Library of Congress, Washington DC.

12. "General Crook Ordaining Spotted Tail Chief of the Sioux at Red Cloud Agency, October 24, 1876." Photograph by Stanley Morrow. Western History Collection, Denver Public Library, Denver CO (X-31746).

of the white people. I know it well, and you can see it plain enough that God Almighty placed those hills there for my wealth, but now you want to take them from me and make me poor, so I ask so much so that I won't be poor."[12]

Perhaps out of frustration with the proceedings, Red Cloud refused the opportunity on his last day in Washington to have his photograph taken with other leaders inside the courtyard of the Patent Office Building. According to a Washington newspaper, this photograph was for the *New York Graphic,* and "Red Cloud declined to join the group, saying that they could have his picture by paying $25 for it."[13] As he had done five years earlier in Brady's studio, Red Cloud used this occasion to protest the government's inattention to his concerns.

Fort Robinson, Nebraska, October 24, 1876

Much trouble swirled around the Lakota reservation during 1876. In the early spring, desirous of controlling the northern Plains, General Philip Sheridan began a three-pronged military campaign against several tribes in the region. In this so-called Great Sioux War, Native American forces won several significant encounters – including the celebrated Battle of the Little Bighorn, in which Custer was killed. Though Red Cloud's son Jack fought in many of these battles, the fifty-five-year-old chief chose not to participate and instead spent the summer at his home. In September, with hostilities having settled down, former Commissioner of Indian Affairs George Manypenny led a group to the Red Cloud Agency to discuss the status of the dis-

puted Black Hills and to press for peace. Forced by authorities to sell or starve, Red Cloud agreed to cede the Black Hills, much to the consternation of those "nonprogressive" Lakota leaders who continued to oppose a negotiated settlement. Plans were also discussed to move the agency again to a new location, two hundred miles east, on the Missouri River.

In October, General George Crook arrived at Fort Robinson, the two-year-old military camp near the Red Cloud Agency, to disarm the remaining militants. In order to undercut Red Cloud's political authority, he proclaimed Spotted Tail the "preeminent chief" of all the Lakotas. Local photographer Stanley J. Morrow accompanied Crook's party, hoping to create a series of views illustrating the recent hostilities on the northern Plains. He had just completed work at the Little Bighorn site and was traveling with Crook in search of images that might document the peace negotiations. One photograph recorded a large group gathered outside a two-story agency building (figure 12). In a light-colored jacket at the center of the group, General Crook stands beside Spotted Tail and restages his proclamation for Morrow's benefit. Red Cloud is the second person to the right of Spotted Tail. Though American authorities invested much significance in Crook's "official" proclamation, it meant little to Red Cloud and other Lakota leaders, who continued to exercise their power as they had done in the past. In the Lakotas' political structure, single individuals did not after all occupy an executive position, as in the American government.

For Morrow, this photograph became the concluding image in a thirty-one-card series titled "Crook's Expedition

13. Red Cloud, 1876. Photograph by Stanley Morrow. Courtesy, National Museum of the American Indian, Smithsonian Institution, Washington DC.

against Sitting Bull, 1876." By placing it last, Morrow signaled that the Great Sioux War was over. Reproduced three months later as an engraving in *Frank Leslie's Illustrated Newspaper*, this image showed the nation that significant changes were afoot on the Plains. Yet peace between American authorities and the Lakotas had not been fully realized. The Hunkpapa leader Sitting Bull remained free, and Spotted Tail's position as defined by Crook was far from secure.

Fort Robinson, Nebraska, December 1876

When Stanley Morrow returned to Fort Robinson in December, he secured an individual portrait of the famous chief. Dressed in a heavy overcoat and holding a hat, Red Cloud stands in front of a log building and looks away from the camera (figure 13). In a letter published in a local Dakota newspaper not long after his return from this trip, Morrow wrote about this encounter: "He seems to take his disposition rather hard, but claims that it will make no difference to his people. Through the kindness of the Indian trader, Mr. Dear, I was enabled to procure some good negatives of Red Cloud, today, it being the first time he ever gave a setting to a photographer."[14] Morrow would not be the last photographer to make this proud yet inaccurate claim.

It is often unclear why Red Cloud posed for a particular photograph. At this time, much confusion surrounded affairs at the Red Cloud Agency. The previous summer's hostilities, the controversial Black Hills treaty, and Crook's intervention had created an uproar throughout the Lakota reservation. Intratribal factions were more pronounced than ever,

14. "Indian Chief, Red Cloud," 1876. Photograph by the Centennial Photographic Company. Historical Society of Pennsylvania, Philadelphia (2613).

and few were ready to abide by Crook's designation of Spotted Tail as leader of the larger nation. Spotted Tail himself was not altogether prepared to serve in this capacity and did little to solidify his newfound position. Perhaps Red Cloud's involvement with Morrow stemmed from the chief's desire to attract attention to himself in order to bolster his standing, since the developments of the past year had compromised his reputation among many tribal members. As it had done in the past, photography might serve as a means of asserting his presence in Lakota political affairs. And in fact, when the dust stirred up by these events had finally settled several months later, Red Cloud remained the leading voice of his people.

Though government officials were intent on undermining his status, Red Cloud remained a mythic figure in the Euro-American imagination and his name continued to be appropriated in various ways. At the Philadelphia Centennial Exposition in the summer of 1876, for example, the Department of the Interior exhibited the results of its work in surveying the lands and researching the Native peoples west of the Mississippi River. Selected for that display were several life-size mannequins of Native individuals, including one identified as Red Cloud (figure 14).[15] Whereas the others were all posed performing domestic duties, the curators placed a warbonnet on the head and a tomahawk in the hand of the Red Cloud mannequin. Even though he had refused to participate in the military campaign of that year, Red Cloud remained, in the eyes of Euro-American society, the ever hostile warrior.[16] As one U.S. Army colonel explained during this same period, the Lakotas "are the most powerful tribe or nation of Indians on this continent, and have always been noted for their freedom of action, impatience under restraint, and bravery in battle, . . . and their greatest warrior is Red Cloud."[17]

The White House, Washington DC, September 27, 1877

At the end of September 1877, Red Cloud made his fourth trip in eight years to Washington. According to the *Wyoming Weekly Leader*, government officials initially opposed this visit because of its high cost and the perceived absence of pressing issues. The newspaper pointedly editorialized that "the government pays the expenses of a lot of barbarians who visit the East for no other purpose than to gratify their vanity and make a useless display of themselves. The visit of the Sioux from Red Cloud and Spotted Tail [Agencies] will accomplish no purpose, and President Hayes will do the country a great service by giving these painted murderers the cold shoulder."[18] Nevertheless, Red Cloud, Spotted Tail, and twenty-three others traveled to Washington to discuss with Indian Bureau officials the proposed resettlement of the Lakotas to lands near the Missouri River and to protest the Black Hills treaty that they had signed the previous year.

Though many governmental authorities opposed funding this delegation, the eastern public was abuzz with excitement about their visit, eager to see representatives of the tribe that had defeated Custer and the Seventh Cavalry the previous summer at the Battle of the Little Bighorn. Custer's remains had recently been buried in a well-publicized ceremony at West Point, and this "massacre" remained an open wound to many Americans.

Interest also stemmed from the controversy surrounding the recent death of Crazy Horse, the famed Oglala warrior whose resistance during the Great Sioux War had made his name a household word throughout the nation. Less than three weeks before Red Cloud's arrival in Washington, Crazy Horse had been knifed to death as he was resisting imprisonment at Fort Robinson. Though Red Cloud had not been there at the time, some believed him partly responsible for this tragedy. Jealous of the young warrior's recent rise in popularity, Red Cloud was said to have spread malicious rumors among government officials about Crazy Horse's supposed intentions, rumors that contributed to the sense of confusion and tension-filled atmosphere in which he was killed. Represented by the American press as a ruthless intratribal power struggle, this event overshadowed the delegation's Washington visit, and much controversy swirled around Red Cloud in the following months.

As in the past, little of an official nature was accomplished during this trip. The party did meet with recently elected President Rutherford B. Hayes on two separate occasions, but Red Cloud's new demands regarding the Black Hills were largely ignored. Likewise, Red Cloud was reluctant to accept the government's proposal to move the Oglala agency eastward

15. Lakota delegation at the White House, 1877. Photograph by Mathew Brady. Library of Congress, Washington DC.

to a location near the Missouri River.

Following their first meeting with President Hayes in the East Room at the White House, Mathew Brady completed two group portraits of members of the delegation. Though his photographic empire had suffered several financial setbacks, Brady was still considered America's preeminent portrait photographer. In the first view, Red Cloud is seated on the far left wearing a full headdress and holding a pipe and beaded pipe bag (figure 15). His body is turned

16. Lakota delegation at the
White House, 1877. Photograph
by Mathew Brady. Library of
Congress, Washington DC.

sideways so that his face is seen only
in profile.

In the second photograph (figure 16),
Red Cloud is sitting second from the left.
His friend Little Wound has moved from
the back row and now sits to his right.
Again, Red Cloud looks away from
Brady's camera.

Secretary of State William B. Evarts,
Secretary of the Interior Carl Schurz, and
General George Crook were also in atten-
dance on this occasion. Neither they nor
the president posed with the delegation,

17. "District of Columbia – Our Indian Allies – Interview of a Delegation of Indian Chiefs with President Hayes, in the East Room of the White House, September 27th." *Frank Leslie's Illustrated Newspaper*, October 13, 1877. Library of Congress, Washington DC.

18. Lakota delegation at the Corcoran Art Gallery, 1877. Photograph by Alexander Gardner. National Anthropological Archives, Smithsonian Institution, Washington DC (3179-C).

yet in the woodcut print based on this photograph and published on the front page of *Frank Leslie's Illustrated Newspaper* two weeks later (figure 17), the engraver included President Hayes and other government officials. The standing Native American figure who greets Hayes in the newspaper image, though, is not Red Cloud, as the accompanying text claims, but rather an unidentified delegate from the back row of the group portrait. The engraver reinterpreted the Brady photograph in order to achieve the newspaper's desired ends. Given the public interest in the Lakota delegation, *Leslie's* was eager to record visually the initial meeting between Hayes and Red Cloud. Since Brady was not able to take that photograph – both because of the technological limitations of the medium and because presi-

dents during this period rarely allowed themselves to be photographed alongside Native leaders – the engraver fulfilled the newspaper's wishes by wielding an intrusive hand. This practice was common in illustrated newspapers of the era.

Corcoran Art Gallery, Washington DC, October 3, 1877

As one photograph by Alexander Gardner reflects, government officials often accompanied Native American groups to significant Washington landmarks and cultural institutions – in this case, the Corcoran Art Gallery (figure 18). Red Cloud stands in the center, between Black Crow and Spotted Tail. He and others wear silver peace medals that Secretary Schurz had given them. During this stay

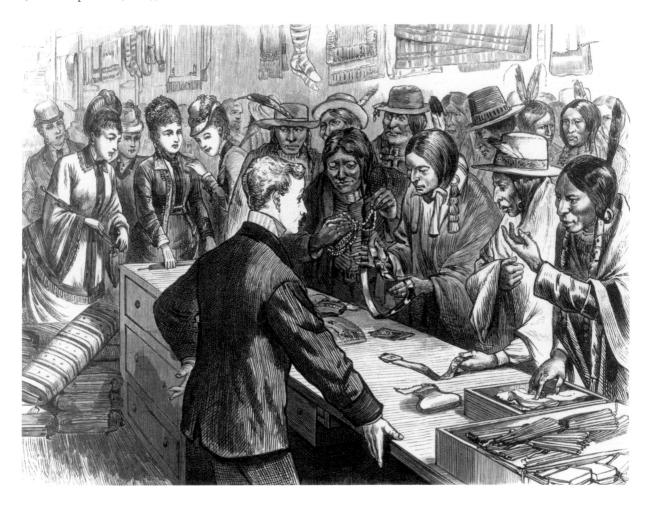

19. "New York City – Our Indian Allies – Sioux Warriors Making Purchases on Broadway for Themselves and Squaws, October 5th." *Frank Leslie's Illustrated Newspaper*, October 20, 1877. Library of Congress, Washington DC.

in Washington, Red Cloud and his party also visited George Washington's tomb at Mount Vernon and attended a performance by William "Buffalo Bill" Cody and his theatrical troupe at Ford's Theater.

Before returning home, the group traveled again to New York City, where they continued their sightseeing by visiting Central Park, an aquarium, and the Museum of Natural History. Government authorities gave each delegation member forty dollars to buy gifts and clothes, and *Leslie's* highlighted the spectacle of their shopping spree along Broadway with the

illustration reproduced in figure 19. According to the accompanying article, "they were taken into several of the largest wholesale and retail establishments, where, as brilliant colors, shining surfaces, and gaudy compositions were placed before them, they grew fairly wild with delight."[19] Red Cloud's participation in such activities is another indication that he was not averse to attention and publicity. Indeed, his experiences in the East and the presents that he brought home with him only added to his public prestige.

2. The Path of Diplomacy, 1877–1880

Within Oglala society the year 1877 marked a profound turning point in political relations with the U.S. government. Red Cloud's reluctant decision the previous year to sign a treaty ceding control of the Black Hills, together with Crazy Horse's sudden death, precipitated widespread changes in the Oglalas' interaction with American authorities. Following the 1868 Fort Laramie treaty, Crazy Horse and other "nonprogressives" had actively resisted negotiations with the United States, deciding instead to pursue military confrontations. In the coming years, however, the Oglala tribal council would choose diplomacy, not war, in an attempt to maintain its political sovereignty and land base – a choice which, as Red Cloud was to learn, was accompanied by much frustration.

Unknown Location, Fall 1877

Daniel Mitchell, a commercial photographer from Deadwood, Dakota Territory, photographed Red Cloud not long after his return from Washington. In this image he wears a feather, has braided his hair, and holds a pipe and beaded pipe bag (figure 20). He also wears the silver peace medal he had recently received in the East.

Later in October, as government officials had hoped, Red Cloud agreed under pressure to the resettlement of the Red Cloud Agency to a site more than two hundred miles to the east on the Missouri River. Reluctant to move again, many tribal members loathed this plan. A tentative compromise was reached, though, one that would allow the issue to be revisited the next spring. Several weeks later, Indian Bureau authorities having promised the Oglalas food and supplies for the winter, a majority of the tribe began the overland trek. Within the Euro-American community the news of this agency's removal was hailed as a great victory. The following passage from an editorial in the *Wyoming Weekly Leader* suggests this excitement:

The weight which is lifted from the hearts of the hardy pioneers who have struggled for years to redeem the vast and fertile plains of Wyoming from the blight of solitude, and the reign of terror caused by the murderous raids of the savage and restless Sioux, cannot be measured by mere words. The safe and speedy removal of these Indians to a point far from our border means the infusing of new life and energy into every industry which thrives on our plains, hills, and valleys. It means the stock grower and the farmer can hereafter roam at will through the rich northland, and, selecting such sections as are best adapted to the purposes of each, there settle down in peace and pursue their vocations, hearing no more the savage whoop of painted demons, and running no risk of losing their scalps, having their herds driven off, or their improvement given to the torch. And so we say: Thank God that Wyoming is free at last.[1]

20. Red Cloud, 1877. Photograph by Daniel S. Mitchell. National Anthropological Archives, Smithsonian Institution, Washington DC (3237-D).

Because of bad weather, insufficient supplies, and low morale, however, the group of some eight thousand did not reach their destination that fall, and over the winter, Red Cloud's ideas about the Oglalas' resettlement changed. When discussions with government officials were renewed the next summer, he adamantly refused to move so far east and demanded that a new site – one chosen by his own people – be considered. Recalling earlier government promises, Red Cloud forced Indian Bureau officials to abandon their proposed plans for a site on the Missouri.[2] Instead, a previously discussed site on the White River was agreed upon. Located fifty miles northeast of the tribe's former home, the new Pine Ridge Agency – renamed by government officials in an effort to downplay the chief's influence – satisfied nearly all involved. For the Oglalas, who had endured three years of negotiations on this topic, a decision concerning their agency was at last final. Now attention could be paid to other concerns.

Unknown Location, Late 1870s

Photographs of subjects as popular as Red Cloud circulated widely. Common industry practices, such as the copying and marketing of best-selling photographs by different studios, contributed to the proliferation of certain images. Though photographers often traded or sold negatives to others, some also stole images outright by rephotographing them. One in particular (figure 21) appeared on the cardboard mounts of at least three different commercial practitioners. The original photographer is not known, but James E. Meddaugh took credit for it.

21. Red Cloud, late 1870s. Photograph by James E. Meddaugh. Nebraska State Historical Society, Lincoln (RG2845:3-4).

Beginning in the late 1880s, Meddaugh ran a photographic studio in Rushville, Nebraska, a small town less than thirty miles from Pine Ridge. Judging by the chief's appearance, though, this portrait was made at least a decade earlier. Indeed, Red Cloud strikes a similar pose and wears an almost identical outfit as in the previous photograph, peace medal included. The only differences appear to be his pipe and the elaborately painted backdrop behind him.

The fact that he holds a pipe in this and other photographs from this period provides additional evidence that Red Cloud understood himself to be performing an important diplomatic role for his people. Within Lakota society the pipe served as the connection between an individual and the spirits who helped to sustain and nurture that person's family and the tribe at large. It also played a central role in council meetings and was often brought out at diplomatic proceedings with outside nations.[3] Though it is not known whether or not this pipe was in fact his own – he was photographed with several different pipes over the course of his life – Red Cloud's decision to hold it signifies a desire to negotiate in good faith with the non-Native world. It also indicates that he saw the ritual of portrait photography as serious business.

Despite the often heated political tensions that existed between the Lakotas and the United States during this period, Red Cloud's interest in being photographed by various local photographers suggests a willingness to maintain a connection with Euro-American society. At a time when Sitting Bull (Hunkpapa) had fled to Canada with his followers, Red Cloud chose photography as one means to continue interactions with the non-Native world.

22. Red Cloud, late 1870s. Photographer unknown. Courtesy, National Museum of the American Indian, Smithsonian Institution, Washington DC.

23. Ulysses S. Grant peace medal owned by Red Cloud, 1871. © Robert S. Peabody Museum of Archaeology, Phillips Academy, Andover MA. All rights reserved.

Unknown Location, Late 1870s

In another portrait from this period (figure 22), Red Cloud wears two peace medals around his neck. Presented to him by government officials during his trips to Washington, these medals represented more than simply gifts to please important visitors.[4] As indicated by the messages and symbols on one medal owned by Red Cloud (reproduced in figure 23), they acted as a declaration of the government's intention to make peace with Native peoples. The depiction of the Bible, a plow, and other farming implements on the medal's reverse reveals the government's desire to transform them into law-abiding Christian farmers.

Red Cloud's decision to wear these medals repeatedly before the camera indicates how much he valued them. Only prominent leaders were presented with such gifts, and the fact that he owned at least two medals certainly pleased him. Interestingly, his embrace of these symbolic tokens parallels his increasing tendency to promote – at least before Euro-American audiences – an accommodationist position with the dominant culture. The following excerpt from a speech that Red Cloud delivered during this period (the exact circumstances are not known) is an eloquent statement of his own disillusionment and his vision for the Oglalas' future:

We have done all we can for ourselves, our wives and children, and have broke our spears, and set down to eat the white man's bread. We know we are paupers, but they made us what we are. . . . The white man's steps are strong and have crushed us, as the grass is crushed by the feet of the buffalo. And why do they build agencies and feed us? Because you know you

have robbed us of all we had; and the white man's God will not let you starve us to death. Your God has saved us. In His name, then, we ask you, a rich and powerful people, to give us what you justly owe us. Give us back our self-reliance; our manhood, and a hope in the future; something to live for. We do not want to be paupers; we want to be men. We have but one way to travel now, and that is the white man's road. Let us have good land that we can farm, and pay us back in seed and tools to farm, and plenty of cows and schools, and then it won't be long until we can take care of ourselves, and be men and women, and our hearts will feel good.[5]

Just as one wonders whether Red Cloud understood the significance of peace medals in the same terms as those who distributed them, so too does such a speech encourage one to question how genuine his commitment to the "white man's road" was. His criticism of American misdeeds and his appeal for increased support during this transitional moment, though, are abundantly clear.

Unknown Location, Late 1870s

As his facial expression in another portrait from this period indicates (figure 24), Red Cloud approached photographic sessions in a deliberately serious manner. Throughout his lifetime, he almost never smiled before the camera. Understanding portrait photography as a formal occasion, he was reluctant to share with the photographer anything other than his carefully composed statesman personality.

A similar directness characterizes his statements concerning the reservation's administration during this period. A letter dated January 14, 1879, from Red Cloud to Alfred B. Meacham, the editor of a pro–Native American reform newspaper called the Council Fire, reveals his efforts at communicating his tribe's desires. As Red Cloud could neither speak English nor write, he presumably dictated it to someone at Pine Ridge Agency, who then forwarded a translation to Meacham. Published under the heading "Straight Talk by a Straight Tongued Sioux Chief," it read,

You wrote me a letter on a card, and asked me if I wanted the military to have charge of the Indians. I have heard a great deal about this, and have wondered why I was not asked this question before. I will now answer you for all my people with one mouth. We do not want the military to have charge of us, and when I tell you that, I do not want to hurt the feelings of good men in the army, for there are some good men there, but there are a great many more that are not the kind of men to lead my people in the road that we are anxious to travel. We want to settle down and get cattle and learn to farm. We want to live in houses, have our children educated and learn the white man's ways of right and wrong. I know the army well, and I know they will never learn us these things. It is not their business. . . . I have no objections to the military in its proper place. Let it attend to those that are making war. It should have nothing to do with people that are at peace and trying to do right. I believe the same Great Spirit made us all, and He don't care whether our skin is red, black, or white. What is good for the white man is good for the rest, and he has no right to stand over us in civil life with a gun, than he had to crack his whip over the back of a negro slave. Your paper is the only one open to our people, and if you wish you shall hear from me again. Very respectfully, Red Cloud.[6]

Though Red Cloud did not always en-dorse the reform efforts of "progressive" Americans such as Meacham, he often used papers like the *Council Fire* to present his views about significant issues. His embrace of the American press was in many respects similar to his engagement with photography. Ever mindful of his public persona, he went to great lengths to have himself both seen and heard.

Red Cloud's outspokenness became in-creasingly common following the ap-pointment of Dr. Valentine T. McGilly-cuddy as Pine Ridge agent in March 1879. Formerly the assistant post surgeon at nearby Fort Robinson, McGillycuddy had just turned thirty at the time of his in-stallation. Throughout his seven-year tenure, he and Red Cloud fought often about a host of issues. McGillycuddy was committed to bringing "civilization" to the Oglalas and took an active role in shaping life on the reservation. His heavy hand upset Red Cloud, who wrote Presi-dent Hayes less than a year after McGilly-cuddy's appointment to ask for his re-moval. Hayes refused the request.

McGillycuddy was no supporter of Red Cloud either. In the biography that Julia McGillycuddy wrote about her husband after his death, she labeled the chief the "usurper-dictator" and complained that he was allied with corrupt individuals both on and off the reservation: "Red Cloud's heart was bad, and with the aid of Little Chief's hostiles he resolved to chal-lenge progress; incited by the worst ele-ment among the squawmen and encour-aged by Eastern sentimentalists, many of whom were members of the [Indian] Ring, he determined to make a last stand against the domination of the Agent and the progressives who supported him."[7]

Studio of Charles Bell, Washington DC, May–June 1880

For three weeks in the spring of 1880, Red Cloud accompanied a group known as the Indian School Committee on a visit to three destinations in the East. Their first stop was Carlisle, Pennsylvania, where former military officer Richard Pratt had opened a boarding school for Native American children: during the fall of 1879 he had recruited sixty boys and twenty-four girls from Pine Ridge and neighbor-ing Rosebud agencies, Red Cloud's grand-son among them. Led by Major William D. Andrus, the head of the Lakota agency known as Yankton, the forty-person In-dian School Committee included both Lakota leaders and many of the parents of the children who had gone east. They visited Carlisle to inspect the school and learn more about the well-being of their children.

Several photographs were taken of in-dividuals in this group and of the delega-tion as a whole but not, curiously, of Red Cloud. He did serve as the leading tribal spokesperson during various all-school convocations, but he remains mysteri-ously unaccounted for in these photo-graphs. His absence might suggest a lack of support for the school were it not that he did praise Pratt on this occasion and then again during two subsequent visits.

In addition to visiting Carlisle, the In-dian School Committee also traveled to Hampton, Virginia, to inspect Samuel Chapman Armstrong's Hampton Normal and Industrial School. Established in April 1868, Hampton was dedicated to educating both Native American and Af-rican American youth.

25. *Left to right:* Red Dog, Little Wound, John Bridgeman, Red Cloud, American Horse, Red Shirt, 1880. Photograph by Charles Bell. National Anthropological Archives, Smithsonian Institution, Washington DC (3238-E).

Before proceeding to Hampton, the delegation first stopped in Washington to meet again with President Hayes and Indian Bureau officials. Their purpose was to complain about McGillycuddy and the recent proposal to permit the construction of railroad tracks across the reservation. As in the past, little was accomplished during these talks. Red Cloud also attended a meeting of local temperance leaders at the city's Masonic Temple, where – his father having died of alcoholism – he spoke out against drink. "It's bad

and will send us all to the devil," he exclaimed to the group.[8]

Before they left Washington, Charles Bell invited the delegation to his photographic studio, and Red Cloud agreed to participate in what turned out to be a lengthy session. In a group portrait (figure 25), Red Cloud (*center*) wears white man's clothing and leather shoes. He also holds a gold-capped cane, a gift of Charles E. Mix, who was a friend from the Indian Bureau.[9] (Like his peace medals, Red Cloud seems to have cherished this cane, as it appears repeatedly in his photographs during the next twenty-five years.) Red Dog and Little Wound are seated to his left, American Horse and Red Shirt to his right. Following convention, the delegation's interpreter, John Bridgeman, stands behind the group.

Despite Red Cloud's statesmanlike bearing and his long familiarity with – and sometimes embrace of – Euro-American society, commercial photographers wanted to maintain the iconographic representation of the Native American. No photographer in Washington was more skillful in creating images that the dominant culture wanted to see and believe than Charles Bell. In his self-described "palatial studio" along Pennsylvania Avenue, "the most celebrated thoroughfare of the national capital," he built the preeminent photographic business in Washington. After Mathew Brady's gallery collapsed because of financial mismanagement, Bell's studio became the place where Indian Bureau officials most routinely brought their business.[10]

Bell was particularly successful at manipulating his subjects to meet his often sensational ends, frequently posing them in front of painted backdrops and outfitting them in elaborate Native costumes. In setting up this photograph (figure 26), Bell has wielded a characteristically intrusive hand, placing Red Cloud in a completely fictionalized setting to create a highly romanticized portrait. A pile of hay lies scattered at his feet (in part to hide his leather shoes); a papier-mâché rock sits beside his chair; a painted seascape hangs behind him. Bell used exactly the same setting in dozens of individual portraits of Native Americans who passed

26. Red Cloud, 1880. Photograph by Charles Bell. Courtesy, National Museum of the American Indian, Smithsonian Institution, Washington DC (N20762).

27. Red Cloud, 1880. Photograph by Charles Bell. National Anthropological Archives, Smithsonian Institution, Washington DC (52836).

through his studio. Furthermore, in order to play up Red Cloud's "Indianness," he has dressed him up in the same tasseled shirt and breastplate that Little Wound wore in the group portrait.

Bell was striving to show that Native Americans still belonged to a primitive culture that remained untouched by the influences of "civilization." As the popularity of his work indicates, those who wished to purchase such portraits much preferred the "wild Indian" to the emasculated reservation dweller living on government rations. This image also suggests that Red Cloud found it increasingly difficult to avoid this sort of manipulation.

At least three other photographs of Red Cloud were taken during this same studio session which, seen together, suggest Bell's interest in creating images that would serve not only commercial ends but specific scientific goals as well. In particular, Bell was supplying photographs of Native American subjects to the new Bureau of American Ethnology in Washington. Inspired in part by William Blackmore's example, the BAE had been established in 1879 to collect, preserve, and study Native American cultures. From the outset, Major John Wesley Powell, its first director, championed the idea of creating a systematic program to collect photographic portraits of Native Americans.

The organizers of this new archive believed that close-up views (as in figure 27) would provide the scientific community with important information about the mental faculties and character of Native Americans; that belief was grounded on the assumption that physiognomy provided this sort of insight. Because of its

ability to make a detailed and permanent visual record, photography became an important tool in their work.[11] Given his age and heroic past, Red Cloud was deemed an especially attractive subject.

The related field of phrenology was also thriving during the nineteenth century, as scientists strove to explain racial difference. Several years later the American Phrenological Institute issued an "Opinion . . . Concerning Red Cloud's Mental Organism," revealing that the chief had also allowed scientists to examine and take measurements of his skull.

The head is large, measuring twenty-three and a half inches around and fifteen from ear to ear over the top. The organs of the social group in the brain are marked in the chart as follows: Amativeness large, Philoprogenitiveness large, Adhesiveness very large, Inhabitiveness very large. He is therefore strong in his attachments to home, friends, wife and children. In the executive region we find Combativeness less developed than Destructiveness or Secretiveness; hence he is naturally pacific, yet possessing the qualities of the successful warrior. He would never go on the war-path through personal ambition or revenge, but as a patriotic duty he would fight to the death. Self-esteem is large, and Approbativeness but moderate, giving dignity and independence of character, self-respect and self-confidence. Firmness is large, as shown by the height of the head; hence the character is stable, and with large Conscientiousness and a fair degree of Hope, we have a man of high purpose, fixed convictions, unyielding devotion to what he believes to be right and duty. The perceptive organs, as in the aboriginal head generally, are all large, forming a beetling cliff above the eyes. Few things worth seeing escape the observation of this man, and his judgment of things is quick and broad. His language is

28. Red Cloud, 1880. Photograph by Charles Bell. National Anthropological Archives, Smithsonian Institution, Washington DC (52837).

evidently active – see the eye expression – and as an orator he is logical, forcible, somewhat poetic, but not wordy or especially rhetorical. He is eloquent, but his eloquence does not depend on the rhetorical arts; it is of the multum in parvo sort, simple yet strong, the kind of oratory which comes direct from a full heart, through an active and strong brain, and goes direct as a plumed arrow to the brains and hearts of auditors.[12]

This pseudoscientific description is characteristic of Euro-American efforts at that time to understand and maintain distinctions between ethnic groups. To acquire images that would give scientists the information necessary to map a subject's skull in three dimensions, the organizers of the BAE archive instructed photographers such as Bell to take pictures from at least two perspectives.[13] In figure 28, Bell has either repositioned his camera or turned Red Cloud sideways to produce a profile view.

One individual who wrote about assembling such a photographic archive was Ferdinand V. Hayden. As the director of the United States Geological Survey, Hayden was charged with mapping western lands and surveying the Native American communities who lived on them. But as he explained, he often had difficulty in getting Native Americans to cooperate.

Those who have never attempted to secure photographs and measurements or other details of the physique of Indians, in short, any reliable statistics of individuals or bands, can hardly realize the obstacles to be overcome. The American Indian is extremely superstitious, and every attempt to take his picture is rendered difficult if not entirely frustrated by his deep-rooted belief that the process places some portion of himself in the power of the white man, and his suspicion that such control may be used to his injury. No prescribed regulations for the taking of photographs, therefore, are likely to be fully carried out. As a rule, front and profile views have been secured whenever practicable. Usually it is only when an Indian is subjected to confinement that those measurements of his person which are suitable for anthropological purposes can be secured. In most cases the Indian will not allow his person to be handled at all, nor submit to any inconvenience whatever. Much tact and perseverance are required to overcome superstitious notions, and in many cases, even of the most noted chiefs of several tribes, no portrait can be obtained by any inducement whatever.[14]*

Red Cloud, by contrast, as it was neither his first nor his last involvement in this sort of scientific project, apparently did not mind being subjected to the scrutiny of the photographer's gaze. The studio session must have lasted at least an hour, yet Red Cloud's facial expression remains almost identical throughout. For him, photography was part of a larger effort to secure specific personal and tribal ends. He received not only money and other gifts but increased attention to himself and the people for whom he spoke. Though photography might not always bring these issues directly to light, his commitment to diplomacy was such that he patiently followed Bell's directions, hopeful that his cooperation might lead to political rewards.

3. Playing the American, 1881–1889

In Agent McGillycuddy, Red Cloud faced one who threatened to overturn the power of the Oglala tribal council. Disturbed by McGillycuddy's heavy-handed program of acculturation, Red Cloud and others contrived new strategies for contesting the dominant culture during the 1880s. As the photographs from this decade indicate, Red Cloud responded to the challenge by taking on many of the customs and costumes of those "civilized" Americans against whom he was battling. Gone were the feathers that he had worn in his hair and other material signs of his "Indianness." In their place, he adopted the appearance and wardrobe of Euro-American society. His apparently sudden turn did not mean that Red Cloud had finally acquiesced to U.S. authorities. Rather, it signaled a creative, yet ultimately futile attempt by the Oglala leader to gain greater autonomy and respect.

Studio of William Cross, Niobrara, Nebraska, 1881–82

With his legs crossed and his body leaning sideways on his chair, Red Cloud strikes a relaxed pose for the local Nebraska photographer William Cross (figure 29). As in many photographs from these years, he is dressed in clothes that a dignified white man might wear – except for the moccasins. In addition to a suit and tie, he wears a gold fob on his vest and holds the same gold-capped cane that Bell photographed him with in 1880.

Red Cloud's decision to dress and pose like a distinguished white man was his way of challenging the prevailing stereotypes of Native Americans. No longer content to be seen as some sort of mythic Indian character, he used this and other occasions in the photographer's studio to assert something about the man that he was. As a diplomat committed to the idea of preserving the Lakotas' political sovereignty, he wanted to be treated with the same respect accorded to other national leaders. Furthermore, he wanted to be the one to make the decisions regarding his tribe's future, rather than some outside individual or institution. In advancing toward that goal, Red Cloud believed it important to look more like those non-Natives with whom he was interacting.

Agent McGillycuddy had a great deal of difficulty working with such an independent-minded leader. Indeed, the feud that existed between the two men was often more about the manner in which decisions were made than about their actual substance. On many issues pertaining to the Oglalas' welfare, including schools, trade, and farming, Red Cloud and McGillycuddy expressed similar thoughts. It was McGillycuddy's desire to lead in shaping the tribe's future and his disregard of the tribal governing structure that caused frequent conflicts with Red Cloud and others. In his annual report to the commissioner of Indian affairs

in 1880, the agent explained that he had
wanted Oglala families to move away
from the Pine Ridge Agency and begin
the process of settling homesteads.

*In inducing them to scatter out in this way, I
have naturally incurred the ill will of some of
the chiefs, as they are fully alive to the fact that
as soon as these Indians become house-owners
and land-owners their glory as petty potentates
will have departed. So I have necessarily met
much opposition, notably from Red Cloud,
who, with the neighboring chief Spotted Tail,
form about as egregious a pair of old frauds in
the way of aids to their people in civilization as
it has ever been my fortune or misfortune to encounter. When these two old men shall have
been finally gathered to their fathers, we can
truly speak of them as good Indians, and only
regret that Providence in its inscrutable way
had so long delayed their departure.*[1]

Believing that the Oglalas could not
enact substantive changes on their own,
McGillycuddy saw their leaders through
the same distorted lens as the majority of
the dominant culture. To him, Red
Cloud's embrace of aspects of Euro-
American culture only showed his increasing vanity and pettiness.

Originally from Omaha, William Cross
ran a commercial photography studio in
Niobrara, Nebraska, specializing in
scenes of Plains Indian life and portraits
like the oval cabinet card in figure 30.
Though he was situated in a small town,
his images circulated widely.

In July 1881 the Hunkpapa leader Sitting Bull and his followers returned from
five years in Canadian exile and surren-
dered to American authorities at nearby
Fort Randall. Forced to flee in the wake of
the Great Sioux War, Sitting Bull had
gained a national reputation as an unre-

30. Red Cloud, 1881 or 1882. Photograph by William Cross. Courtesy, National Museum of the
American Indian, Smithsonian
Institution, Washington DC.

31. "'Forbear,' I cried, striking up the levelled barrel." Illustration from William F. Butler, *Red Cloud, the Solitary Sioux: A Story of the Great Prairie* (London: S. Low, Marston, Searle & Rivington, 1882).

deemable Native warrior. Consequently, the American public celebrated his surrender as "reliev[ing] the northwestern territory of its only terror," as one newspaper editorialized. It then speculated that "the great chief will probably end his career as an attraction in some show" – as, indeed, he did.[2]

This event, among others, continued to color the manner in which non-Natives perceived all Native leaders. However accustomed Red Cloud had grown to interacting within Euro-American society, national and international audiences still understood him as the epitome of the noble savage. Two engravings representative of this imagined identity (figures 31 and 32) were published in an 1882 romantic adventure novel, *Red Cloud, The Solitary Sioux: A Story of the Great Prairie*, by the English author William F. Butler. The illustrations highlight two episodes from this fictitious tale in which Red Cloud agrees to guide a group of Englishmen hunting on the Great Plains. Throughout the book, Butler describes Red Cloud as one of the last of his race, but in the public eye he remained the fierce warrior, ever battling against the encroaching white man.

Unknown Location, 1882

Even though most perceived him to be a fiery warrior hostile to all non-Natives, Red Cloud often went out of his way to be cooperative – even generous. When the Ponca tribe was displaced from its homelands, Red Cloud and other Native leaders traveled to Washington in August 1881 and (successful for once) negotiated an arrangement that transferred more than twenty-five thousand acres of the Great

32. "'Look,' said Red Cloud, 'there is the yellow dust for which the white man fights, and robs, and kills.'" Illustration from William F. Butler, *Red Cloud, the Solitary Sioux: A Story of the Great Prairie* (London: S. Low, Marston, Searle & Rivington, 1882).

Sioux Reservation to the Poncas. Declaring that "I love all men now," Red Cloud recommended that "these poor people. . . . live at my agency. All of my Indians wish it. Our hearts are large, our will is good." And although government officials were willing to compensate the Lakotas for these lands, Red Cloud refused to discuss the subject.[3]

During the latter half of his life, Red Cloud also established and maintained many friendships outside the reservation. Seated beside him in this photograph (figure 33) is Charles P. Jordan, one of his closest white friends. Over the years of their relationship, which lasted until Red Cloud's death in 1909, Jordan worked in various capacities on the Pine Ridge and Rosebud reservations.

Though they may have known each other earlier, their friendship grew out of a crisis at Pine Ridge involving McGillycuddy during the summer of 1882. At that time, Red Cloud was campaigning hard for the agent's removal; likewise, McGillycuddy was intent on bending Red Cloud to his will. After one exchange of provocations, McGillycuddy ordered Red Cloud to be arrested and incarcerated. The impasse between the two men was finally broken when Red Cloud backed down and ordered his followers to disarm. While locked in the guardhouse, he also asked his son Jack to raise the American flag over his house as a gesture of peace and goodwill, a conciliatory move that brought him renewed support among many non-Natives who opposed McGillycuddy's administration.

In the following months the thirty-one-year-old Jordan served as a member of the investigative team responsible for reporting this incident to the Indian Bureau. Ultimately, the investigation exonerated Red Cloud and exposed serious questions regarding McGillycuddy's ability to serve as agent to the Oglalas. Yet McGillycuddy remained entrenched in his position.

The friendship between Jordan and Red Cloud was further solidified when Jordan later married one of Red Cloud's nieces, Julia Walks First. Although the circumstances behind this photograph are unclear, it is the first of several occasions when Red Cloud posed with Jordan. Each man wears a formal suit, and Red Cloud again clutches his prized gold-capped cane. Their interpreter stands behind them.

Studio of John N. Choate, Carlisle, Pennsylvania, December 1882

In December 1882, Red Cloud made his seventh trip east to meet with officials, this time traveling only with his interpreter, Ed Laramie. Red Cloud announced at the outset of the trip that he was seeking $10,000 from the government in compensation for the loss of horses during the Great Sioux War six years earlier.[4] Given the events of the previous summer, however, he was also interested in furthering his campaign against McGillycuddy.

On his way to Washington, he stopped once more at Carlisle, Pennsylvania, to visit Pratt's school for Native American children. This was Red Cloud's third visit, but it was the first time he agreed to pose for John N. Choate, the school's official photographer. From the start of his educational endeavor, Pratt had regarded photography as a means to help ensure the school's success. Not only could it

33. *Left to right*: Red Cloud, interpreter, Charles P. Jordan, 1882. Photographer unknown. National Anthropological Archives, Smithsonian Institution, Washington DC (3237-G).

document the "progress" that Native children made under his guidance, but sending photographs back to the reservations from which his students came proved to be "the best way of keeping parents happy."[5] Pratt also incorporated Choate's photographs in the school's promotional materials, which he often sent to important benefactors and potential patrons.

In this photograph (figure 34), Red Cloud sits beside Edward B. Townsend, a government official assigned to investigate reports of corruption and abuse within the Indian Bureau; Ed Laramie stands behind the two men. Townsend had visited Pine Ridge earlier that fall, where he confirmed reports of McGillycuddy's fraudulent administration. He had joined Red Cloud en route to Washington and agreed to pose with him during their visit to Carlisle. In this group portrait, Red Cloud has crossed his arms and seems to stare rather coldly out at Choate. He again wears a white man's suit and leather shoes, and has affixed a small pin or tie tack to his cravat. Like the photograph with Jordan, this image reveals that he willingly posed alongside non-Native men he respected. Such sessions helped to solidify relationships that were important to Red Cloud. Indeed, Townsend proved to be a useful ally in his campaign against McGillycuddy.

34. *Left to right:* Red Cloud, Ed Laramie (interpreter), Agent Edward B. Townsend, 1882. Photograph by John Nicholas Choate. Cumberland County Historical Society, Carlisle PA.

The most remarkable change recorded in the several photographs taken by Choate at Carlisle is that Red Cloud has cut his long hair to a point above his shoulders. The close-up view in figure 35 seems to highlight this recent act. Lakota men during the nineteenth century devoted much attention to their hair, most of them preferring to grow it well below their shoulders and often braiding it, as several earlier photographs of Red Cloud indicate. The Lakotas took such pride in long hair that they sometimes even added artificial hair to secure greater length.[6]

Perhaps Red Cloud decided to cut his hair as a sign of mourning for the death of a close friend or relative, a practice common in Lakota society. Or perhaps he was trying to appear more like a white man by wearing his hair in a Euro-American style. (One of the first things that students at Carlisle faced upon arriving on campus was a trip to the school barber.) For a decade he had preferred clothes made off the reservation, so it is likely that he was now taking another step toward fashioning himself in the manner of a dignified white man. Red Cloud continued to wear his hair short for the next seven years. Notably, it was not until 1890, at a time when many Lakotas were becoming involved with the Ghost Dance, that he let his hair grow out again.

Contemporary observations support the idea that he cut his hair to appear more "gentlemanly." His friend Charles Jordan later wrote that Red Cloud "was very particular as to his personal appearance and long before other Indians would do so, he had his long black hair cut short and he dressed like a gentle-

35. Red Cloud, 1882. Photograph by John Nicholas Choate. Cumberland County Historical Society, Carlisle PA.

36. Red Cloud, 1882. Photograph by John Nicholas Choate. Cumberland County Historical Society, Carlisle PA.

man. And no gentleman was ever more naturally courteous to all whom he met, or more considerate and reverential to the ladies."[7]

It should also be noted that during this period, Red Cloud and his family were baptized by his reservation's recently arrived Roman Catholic priest, Father Joseph Buschmann. Ever since McGillycuddy's appointment to Pine Ridge, he and Red Cloud had quarreled about the latter's wish to allow Catholic missionaries on the reservation. As French Jesuits had worked among the Lakotas for more than two centuries, Red Cloud had long been partial to the Catholic church. Yet, because government officials in Washington had alloted missionary responsibility at Pine Ridge to the Episcopal Church, McGillycuddy refused at first to consider Red Cloud's request; not until 1881 was the restriction lifted. Red Cloud perhaps was also expressing his support for Buschmann by cutting his hair. During this period he complied at least publicly with pronouncements from the Catholic Church, including even its decree that the Oglalas discontinue their annual Sun Dance, one of their most important religious ceremonials.[8]

In another photograph from Carlisle, Red Cloud stands before Choate holding his black felt hat in one hand and his overcoat in the other (figure 36), looking very much like an official visitor to the school. To those who were advocating the "civilization" of the Indian, such an image presented the chief as a model of acculturation.[9]

During his stay at Carlisle, Red Cloud spoke to the students at an all-school convocation – as he had during his two previous visits – and Pratt sponsored a

writing contest in which students were asked to respond to the speech. Luther Standing Bear, a fourteen-year-old Oglala boy, won this contest and its three-dollar prize; his essay was published in the *Morning Star*, the monthly school newspaper, and a month later in the Carlisle town paper. There is no copy of Red Cloud's speech, but according to the winning essay, the chief praised the work being done at the school.[10]

Red Cloud also visited the Hampton Normal and Industrial School in Virginia again, and the published translation of his remarks before the faculty and students there further indicates his public support of these boarding schools: "This is the second time I have come to Hampton. I am very glad to see you here. The work here, we like. We are Indians, but this is what I want you to learn; such as wagon-making, farming, and the other work. We want you to learn this because you will find it a benefit to you. You see that man standing there [school principal Samuel Chapman Armstrong] – who has charge of you. I want you to listen to all he says. He has brains, he has eyes, he will take good care of you. I like all his work, and I am glad to see it."[11]

Though remaining loyal to his tribe and committed to justice on its behalf, Red Cloud seems to have become not necessarily more accommodating but rather more willing to advance the cause of his people by other than traditional means. Embracing photography had been for more than ten years one manifestation of his creativity in negotiating relationships and agreements with Euro-American society. Cutting his hair and lending his support to the boarding school movement were other expressions of his desire

to build bridges with wider constituencies.

Yet Red Cloud adopted a much different, less cooperative attitude with those who showed him little respect. McGillycuddy's annual reports to the commissioner of Indian affairs described Red Cloud as a persistent obstructionist. In 1885 he wrote, "In marked contrast to this majority [of Oglalas who supported the agent], however, is Red Cloud and his immediate closely congregated band and scattered retainers among other bands, who with the support and sympathy of a few misguided or scheming white people in Washington and elsewhere, are as determined as ever in their opposition to schools, farming, stock-raising, and civilization generally."[12]

The fact is that throughout his life, Red Cloud was continually taking on different public personas. This chameleonlike personality was all part of his ongoing negotiation with leaders in both Euro-American and Oglala society. Though some, like McGillycuddy, considered him vainglorious and duplicitous, Red Cloud's actions were always designed to promote the larger goals of his people: namely, Lakota political sovereignty and the procurement of resources necessary to sustain his tribe.

Studio of Frank A. Bowman, New Haven, Connecticut, January 22, 1883

In January 1883, Red Cloud and Laramie traveled to New Haven to visit Othniel C. Marsh, a Yale University professor of paleontology whom Red Cloud had met and made friends with nine years earlier. While digging for fossils in the Dakota Territory in 1874, Marsh observed and later reported to government officials and newspapers in the East the deplorable conditions and widespread corruption on the Lakota reservation.[13] Marsh soon found himself embroiled in a heated controversy between Lakota supporters and Indian Bureau officials, the end result of which was the dismissal of Secretary of the Interior Columbus Delano and Commissioner of Indian Affairs Edward P. Smith. Red Cloud and Marsh remained friends thereafter, often sending each other gifts.

As Marsh declared to a *New York Times* reporter, Red Cloud's trip to New Haven was simply a "friendly visit" and had "nothing to do with politics, matters of Indian policy, or anything of that nature."[14] He greeted Red Cloud at the New Haven train station amid a large crowd of curious onlookers and, during their weekend together, gave his guest a tour of various sites, including the Peabody Museum of Natural History, the Yale University Art Gallery, and the Winchester Armory. They also attended William Gilbert and Arthur Sullivan's newest operetta, *Iolanthe*, during which, according to a news report, they "attracted considerable attention from the audience."[15]

The two began their second day together by visiting Frank A. Bowman's photographic studio. A reporter for the *New Haven Register* recorded the details of that session:

The Sioux chief with his interpreter and Professor Marsh arrived at the photographic establishment at 10:30 o'clock. The subordinates of the place were in a pleasant state of excitement over Red Cloud's visit. They had only a short view of the party however, to fill the measure of their curiosity, as Prof. Marsh hurried Red

37. *Left to right:* Othniel Marsh, Red Cloud, Ed Laramie, 1883. Photograph by Frank A. Bowman. Yale Collection of Western Americana, Beinecke Rare Book and Manuscript Library, New Haven CT.

Cloud upstairs to the studio. No outsiders were permitted to enter while they were there, even a brother professor to Mr. Marsh being compelled to wait downstairs until the sitting was over. It lasted from 10:30 until 12:15 o'clock. Eight or ten sittings were had. Red Cloud posed in a number of postures – full length and half length, full face and side views – and several impressions of the party as a group were taken. In one of the group pictures Red Cloud, Prof. Marsh, and his interpreter were represented as smoking clay pipes in a state of perfect amity, according to the Indian idea.[16]

Dressed in the same outfit that he had worn in Choate's Carlisle studio, Red Cloud stands between Marsh and Laramie in this group portrait (figure 37). That each holds a pipe, including the Yale professor, illustrates Red Cloud and Marsh's mutual respect.

The reporter from the *New Haven Register* later asked Bowman how he "got on with [his] strange customer," to which Bowman answered,

Splendidly. I took him individually and the group collectively in almost every posture that could be thought of. I feared that Red Cloud would be a difficult subject to handle, but he was not. On the contrary, he was much more patient and civilized than the ordinary customer which we have to deal with. If I told him through his interpreter to stand in a certain position, he would stand there as rigid and immovable as a post until his interpreter gave him the word to move. Through the whole ordeal he showed a spirit of the utmost patience, and only seemed anxious to do what I wanted him to do. I imagine he would still be standing in certain positions in which he had been placed, provided he had not been given permission or notice to move. As stoical and expres-

sionless as he was in his ordinary demeanor, I noticed that he was very quick to obey any look or gesture that I gave for his guidance. He always responded by fixing his look on the place indicated and in doing so looked at me with a half-smile and a peculiar expression of intelligence. It said as plain as anything could that he knew what I wanted him to do, and was very pleased to know that he had succeeded in doing it.

Bowman's remarks reflect Red Cloud's long acquaintance with the ritual of portrait photography – a fact that Marsh, despite their long friendship, was apparently not familiar with, according to his remarks quoted in this same article: "I did not care to have reporters or outsiders in the gallery for fear that their presence would disconcert Red Cloud, who is really quite nervous, although you would not judge so from his appearance. He has faced the camera once before – in Washington – and was not at all inclined to sit today. He only did so because I was anxious to have him."[17] In fact, this session actually marked at least the sixteenth time that Red Cloud had posed for a photographer.

In one portrait, Red Cloud shakes hands with Marsh – as he had with William Blackmore eleven years earlier (figure 8) – and together, they hold a ceremonial pipe (figure 38). In the coming years, Red Cloud would pose shaking hands with other Native and non-Native leaders. On each occasion he was interested in marking his friendship with a significant other for the larger public to see.

This studio session was not only an important commemoration of Red Cloud's visit but also an opportunity for Bowman to create a marketable product. During

38. Red Cloud with Othniel Marsh, 1883. Photograph by Frank A. Bowman. Courtesy of Peabody Museum of Natural History, Yale University, New Haven CT.

39. Red Cloud, 1883. Photograph by Frank A. Bowman. Courtesy of Peabody Museum of Natural History, Yale University, New Haven CT.

the late nineteenth century there was much enthusiasm for collecting *cartes de visite* and, later, cabinet cards of famous individuals. Marsh himself sent copies of selected photographs from these sittings as gifts to friends.

Bowman went to great lengths to figure Red Cloud in a manner that would appeal to his clientele. The pipe and pipe bag included in figure 39 and other photographs are one obvious sign of his desire to give these images an air of the Wild West. Interestingly, however, neither object belonged to Red Cloud, nor was the pipe bag even a product of a Lakota artist. As the director of Yale's Peabody Museum, Marsh was the individual responsible for providing these items.

That Red Cloud was willing at times to hold such props reveals that he often deliberately mimicked American customs in portraits from this period. He intended not to harmonize with the culture in which he found himself but rather to maintain a position both inside and outside that world. His decision to wear white man's clothes and to cut his hair reflects a strategic turn in his confrontation with American authorities. Through photography, Red Cloud was able to keep his newly "civilized" face before the American public. Yet at the same time he remained committed to his own set of principles. It is not enough to think in terms of such simple binary oppositions as resistance and accommodation in analyzing Red Cloud's engagement with white America. Instead, his example suggests the creative ways in which a marginalized individual or group can negotiate a relationship with the dominant social order.

40. Red Cloud, 1883. Photograph by Frank A. Bowman. Courtesy of Peabody Museum of Natural History, Yale University, New Haven CT.

Like Charles Bell in Washington, Bowman was interested in creating images not only for the public but for the scientific community in New Haven. Indeed, Marsh purchased $130 worth of photographs from Bowman for the Peabody Museum, many of them enlargements that showed off Red Cloud's physiognomy in great detail.[18] One profile portrait (figure 40) continues the tradition of viewing a Native subject from a variety of perspectives, thus providing scientists with a visual map of the skull. Further, newspaper reports indicate that a phrenologist again measured Red Cloud's head during this particular stay in the East.[19] As much as he was a friend, Red Cloud was also a specimen to Marsh and others.

Before returning home, Red Cloud stopped off in Washington, where, among other things, he spoke through an interpreter before the House Appropriations Committee. Though he had much to complain of in his ongoing rivalry with McGillycuddy, he confined these remarks to an issue that had long upset him: namely, the loss of more than six hundred horses during the summer of 1876. Having finished his speech, he handed the committee a letter explaining his grievances in writing. It read: "LAW CHIEFS – I am an Indian. Look at me. My name is Red Cloud. I have sense. The government through General Crook in 1876 took wrongfully 605 horses from me and my people. I have sense. So have my people. I represent them. I am in debt. I have a large family. Secretary [of the Interior Henry M.] Teller asks me to take cows for my horses. If the government gives me all the cows they have promised, I will have more than we can milk. I am a man

of sense. I want money to pay my debts. Law chiefs, pay me not in cows, but in cash. I am at peace. Let us remain thus."[20]

The photographs taken during this trip east reflect Red Cloud's desire to be seen in exactly these terms: only as a "man of sense" who was "at peace" did he think that he could achieve his specific ends. Yet this often meant going along with the sometimes uncomfortable demands of Euro-American society. Such was the predicament in which he found himself.

Johnson Brothers' Studio, Washington DC, March 1885

In November 1884, Grover Cleveland defeated James Blaine in the presidential election, the first Democrat to win the White House since before the Civil War. Consequently, many people expected sweeping changes to occur in both public policy and government personnel.

Aware of this new atmosphere in Washington, Red Cloud arranged to travel east again in the spring of the following year, as he had done in 1877 after Rutherford B. Hayes's election. He wanted to meet Cleveland and relate to him his tribe's concerns. McGillycuddy tried to prevent it, but Red Cloud made the trip anyway and was able to arrange an appointment with the new president. Despite the troubles back on the reservation, Red Cloud arrived in Washington cautiously optimistic about his prospects. As he remarked at a reception held for him,

This is the eighth time I have visited the city of the Great Father. I am always glad to come here because I always meet good friends here.

41. Red Cloud, 1885. Photograph by Johnson Brothers. Courtesy of South Dakota State Historical Society – State Archives, Pierre.

Everytime I come I find more friends than before. This makes my heart glad. My people have been under a dark cloud for a long time, but I think the sun will shine on us again after a while. Since I first made a treaty with the Government, seventeen years ago, I have kept the law. I promised to walk in the white man's road, and lead my people into the white man's road. I have tried to do it; but sometimes the agents sent me by the Great Father have been in my way and have kept my people back.[21]

Red Cloud and Cleveland met on March 18, the president's forty-eighth birthday; the Oglala chief was about to turn sixty-four. According to the *Washington Post*, during their meeting Red Cloud "complained bitterly of his treatment by Agent McGillycuddy and asked for his removal. The president lent an attentive ear to all he had to say, and promised to give the matter his early attention."[22]

Faithful to his word, Cleveland called McGillycuddy to Washington several weeks later to answer Red Cloud's charges. With Red Cloud present, a hearing was held before the commissioner of Indian affairs. At that time, Colonel George Manypenny, a former Indian Bureau commissioner who had served as a peace negotiator during the Great Sioux War in 1876, testified against McGillycuddy. In the end, nevertheless, the panel took no action against the agent, and McGillycuddy returned to his post at Pine Ridge.

As he had done on almost every previous visit to Washington, Red Cloud made his way to a photographer's studio during this stay. The *Council Fire's* new editor, Thomas A. Bland, was the one responsible for bringing Red Cloud before the camera of Frank R. and J. Orville Johnson. Having visited Pine Ridge the previous summer – only to be arrested and ordered off the reservation by Agent McGillycuddy – Bland was one of Red Cloud's most vocal advocates, and his newspaper played a critical part in publicizing McGillycuddy's abuses. In addition to posing for several individual portraits, Red Cloud agreed to pose with Bland and his wife, Cora, another instance of his desire to formalize relationships with those whom he respected as friends. For the next year, Bland advertised the sale of these photographs through his newspaper.[23]

In one of these portraits (figure 41), Red Cloud wears a white man's suit and bowtie, gifts of the new secretary of the interior, Lucius Quintus Cincinnatus Lamar. His hair remains short, and he holds a dark felt hat that partially obscures the fake rock he stands beside. He may have positioned his hat in this way on purpose; given the "primitive" associations surrounding such a studio prop, he was perhaps uncomfortable next to it. This possibility, together with the fact that Red Cloud neither holds nor wears any Native American objects in this portrait, suggests his desire to be seen on equal terms with the government officials with whom he was interacting.

Studio of John Nephew, Washington DC, April 1889

When Red Cloud entered John Nephew's Washington studio in the spring of 1889, it had been four years since his last trip east. In that interval, much had happened in relations between the Lakotas and the U.S. government. Of particular satisfac-

42. Red Cloud with Charles P. Jordan, 1889. Photograph by John Nephew. National Anthropological Archives, Smithsonian Institution, Washington DC (3243-B-1).

tion for Red Cloud, Agent McGillycuddy had finally been relieved of his duties in May 1886, following yet another government investigation into misconduct on the Pine Ridge Reservation. After years of bitter feuding, Red Cloud could finally claim victory over his longtime nemesis. During a Fourth of July celebration in Chadron, Nebraska, two months later, Red Cloud spoke optimistically about the future: "We came here as two nations, with different hearts and different minds, but today we must become as one nation with but one heart and one mind. We will build our two houses into one. We have been traveling two different roads, let us from now on travel even."[24]

His hopefulness was short-lived. Not long after McGillycuddy's dismissal the Oglalas learned of a new and much greater challenge, one that threatened both their land base and the basic tenets of their society: in February 1887, President Cleveland signed into law the General Allotment Act (also known as the Dawes Act, after the Massachusetts senator who sponsored it), a bill designed to break Native Americans of their belief in communal land ownership. Deemed by government officials and reformers alike as a "progressive" piece of legislation, the act established a system whereby Native families could claim individual ownership of up to 160 acres of land. As Commissioner of Indian Affairs Hiram Price exclaimed at the time, allotment would teach "the Indians habits of industry and frugality, and stimulate them to look forward to a better and more useful life."[25] The act would also relieve the federal government of large and increasingly burdensome appropriations.

At the same time, Indian Bureau officials were eager to sign a new treaty with the Lakotas that would effectively divide up the Great Sioux Reservation, carving out six smaller reservations and freeing thousands of acres for American settlers. Red Cloud, though he now served only as the titular head of the Oglalas, was outspoken in his opposition to both these new developments. Several times he wrote the commissioner of Indian affairs requesting permission to visit Washington to voice his concerns. Each time, however, Indian Bureau officials told him to stay where he was, even when in October 1888 the Brulé leader Gall led a delegation to Washington to oppose the land treaty. For the first time in twenty years, Red Cloud had been shut out of these political negotiations. Lacking official permission to take part, he remained behind.

When President Cleveland signed the new land treaty in March 1889, however, Red Cloud could no longer stand idly by and watch these events unfold. Despite being told by government authorities to remain at Pine Ridge, he set out for Washington the next month, accompanied by his old friend Charles Jordan (see figure 42) and an interpreter named Nicholas Jarvis.

43. Red Cloud with Charles P. Jordan, 1889. Photograph by John Nephew. Western History Collection, Denver Public Library, Denver CO (X-33923).

In a second view that Nephew took of the two friends, Jordan again strikes a relaxed pose, resting his arm on Red Cloud's shoulder (figure 43). Though it is similar in most regards to Nephew's first image, the two men have rearranged themselves before the camera. Red Cloud now wears a handkerchief around his neck and has buttoned his dress jacket. In addition, he sits on a different chair. Jordan has likewise buttoned his jacket, wears the wide-brimmed hat he previously carried, and turns away from the camera slightly. It is not known whether these changes were the photographer's suggestions or decisions on the part of Red Cloud and Jordan, but they do suggest the deliberateness with which these portraits were completed.

Red Cloud continued to wear white man's clothes during this trip, and his hair is cut even shorter than in 1885. This personal style was not favored by most Lakota men of the time. According to ethnographic reports, the Lakotas had been hesitant to adopt white man's dress after their settlement on reservations; as late as 1880, fewer than one-third had chosen to wear the cloth shirts and pants that were increasingly being made available by traders and Indian Bureau agents. Even fewer wore their hair short.[26] Red Cloud's decision to present himself in this manner is thus a deliberate movement away from his tribe's stylistic norms. Furthermore, not since his time in Charles Bell's studio nine years earlier had he worn his chief's feather. By mimicking the fashions of American society, Red Cloud was both experimenting with the idea of being a part of that culture and simultaneously using this posture to further his own personal and political ends.

By contrast, Jordan's hair now falls down past his shoulders, and he has grown a fashionable mustache and goatee. As a westerner in the East, Jordan seems to be interested in reshaping his own persona to meet the romantic expectations of easterners. Indeed, his appearance closely resembles that of William "Buffalo Bill" Cody, the much celebrated entertainer whose Wild West Show was thrilling audiences throughout the nation. Though equally concerned about his public image, Red Cloud used his trips to Washington and these sittings in the photographer's studio to challenge the rose-tinted rendition of western affairs that Cody's show presented.

John Nephew's short-lived commercial studio at 493 Pennsylvania Avenue was located on the same block as Charles Bell's much larger photographic business. Though Red Cloud had worked with Bell nine years earlier, he ended up for whatever reason at Nephew's gallery on this occasion. Nephew represented at least the fifth different Washington photographer for whom Red Cloud had posed. Apparently, neither the Indian Bureau nor Red Cloud had an exclusive arrangement with one particular studio; instead, photographers vied with one another for this potentially lucrative business.

Whereas the previous two photographs affirm Red Cloud and Jordan's friendship, figures 44 and 45 – front and profile closeups – indicate that Nephew regarded Red Cloud as a subject of scientific study. This session marked at least the third time in a decade that Red Cloud's face had been appropriated in this way. Given the weighty issues that the Lakotas were confronting at the time, Red Cloud exudes great patience in Nephew's studio. By dis-

44. Red Cloud, 1889. Photograph by John Nephew. National Anthropological Archives, Smithsonian Institution, Washington DC (3238-A).

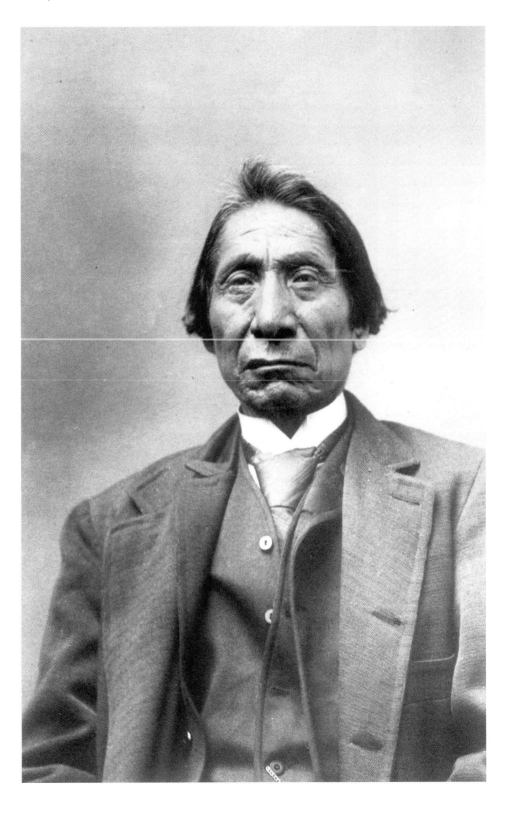

45. Red Cloud, 1889. Photograph by John Nephew. National Anthropological Archives, Smithsonian Institution, Washington DC (3238-B).

playing his "man of sense" persona to American authorities, he hoped to win support for his concerns – and his negotiations with Indian Bureau officials in 1889 did yield one victory: after years of argument about compensation for the loss of horses in 1876, Congress agreed to pay the Oglalas $28,200. Given the hardships they were then suffering, brought by a series of harsh winters and dry summers, this money was an important windfall.

Red Cloud was unable, however, to make serious inroads in renegotiating the proposed land treaty. When a commission led by General George Crook visited Pine Ridge later that summer to seek the signatures of Lakota leaders on this treaty, Red Cloud and others continued to speak out against it, even though a growing faction of Oglala men, led by American Horse, had become more open to accepting the proposal because of its promise to provide much-needed financial assistance. Severe weather on the northern Plains had made the Lakotas desperate for food and other provisions. Eventually, American Horse's voice prevailed, and in December 1889 a Lakota delegation traveled to Washington to sign the treaty. Having broken off relations with American Horse over this issue, Red Cloud remained behind.

The assistance promised under terms of the new treaty was slow in materializing, however, and as a result, many died that winter from disease and starvation. Adding insult to injury, American homesteaders began to make their way onto Lakota lands within months of the treaty's adoption. The influx of settlers angered tribal members and led to occasional outbursts of violence. Many on both sides began to fear a full-blown war.

4. Wounded Knee and Its Aftermath, 1889–1897

46. Red Cloud with Louis John Frederick Iaeger (*left*) and John Maher, 1889. Photograph by George Trager and Fred Kuhn. Dawes County Historical Society, Chadron NE.

The breakup of the Great Sioux Reservation in 1889 was a bitter defeat for Red Cloud. The tremendous loss of land associated with this new agreement extinguished any faint hope he still harbored of maintaining tribal autonomy. Furthermore, having been largely shut out of the treaty negotiations, Red Cloud had grown profoundly disillusioned with the political process. Reduced government aid, worsening conditions on the Oglala reservation, and the destruction of the Great Plains buffalo herd only deepened his despair. These circumstances explain Red Cloud's slow movement during this period away from the public persona that he had maintained during the 1880s. They also provide a historical context for understanding the tragic events that unfolded on the banks of Wounded Knee Creek in December 1890.

Studio of George Trager and Fred Kuhn, Chadron, Nebraska, July 4, 1889

In the summer of 1889, George Trager and Fred Kuhn opened a commercial photographic studio in Chadron, Nebraska, a growing town only thirty miles south of Pine Ridge. Hoping to expand their business, Kuhn moved to Crawford, Nebraska, the following spring to set up a branch office with Trager's brother Ernest. They advertised themselves as "Wigwam Photographers" to emphasize their specialization in Native American portraiture.[1]

Pictured in figure 46 with Red Cloud are Louis John Frederick Iaeger (on the left) and John Maher, two local residents with whom he had made friends on an earlier visit to Chadron. For several years Red Cloud and other tribal members had joined the Fourth of July festivities in Chadron, marching in the annual Main Street parade, performing Native dances, and participating in horse races. Red Cloud was frequently invited to give a speech, too.[2] It was during one of these celebrations that he had met Iaeger and Maher, both of whom worked in the county courthouse. As they were also members of the event's planning committee, the two men often interacted with Red Cloud and other Native leaders. On this occasion, Iaeger arranged for the visit to Trager and Kuhn's studio.[3]

Red Cloud's willingness to pose with these two men at a time of increased tensions between the Lakotas and the U.S. government reveals his continued desire to maintain contacts with non-Natives. Many Lakotas would turn in the coming months to the Ghost Dance, a pan-Indian messianic movement that prophesied the disappearance of Euro-American society and a return to traditional tribal ways. Several years later, Red Cloud spoke about the despair that pervaded the Oglala reservation at this time and led many of his people to join the Ghost Dance movement:

*We felt that we were mocked in our misery. We
had no newspapers and no one to speak for us.
We had no redress. Our rations were again reduced. You who eat three times each day, and
see your children well and happy around you,
can't understand what starving Indians feel.
We were faint with hunger and maddened by
despair. We held our dying children, and felt
their little bodies tremble as their souls went
out and left only a dead weight in our hands.
They were not very heavy, but we ourselves
were very faint, and the dead weighed us down.
There was no hope on earth, and God seemed to
have forgotten us. Some one had again been
talking of the Son of God, and said He had
come. The people did not know; they did not
care. They snatched at the hope. They screamed
like crazy men to Him for mercy. They caught
at the promises they heard He had made.*[4]

Red Cloud himself, however, remaining dedicated to the idea that dialogue
rather than separation was vital to his
nation's future welfare, never participated in the Ghost Dance.

Studio of George Trager, Chadron, Nebraska, 1890–91

As the portraits in figures 47 and 48 indicate, Red Cloud began to let his hair grow
out not long after his return from Washington in 1889. The decision to abandon
the shorter hairstyle suggests his disillusionment with non-Native officials and
his growing desire to reengage with traditional Oglala customs. In light of the
difficulties at this time surrounding conditions on the reservation and political
affairs with the federal government, he
may have felt that his cause would be
better served if he embraced an outward
appearance more in keeping with conven-

47. Red Cloud, 1890 or 1891. Photograph by George Trager. Western History Collection, Denver
Public Library, Denver co (x-
31322).

48. Red Cloud, 1890 or 1891. Photograph by George Trager. National Anthropological Archives, Smithsonian Institution, Washington DC (3237-H).

tional Oglala habits. Never again did he return to wearing his hair short for any extended period of time, perhaps a sign of his exasperation with Euro-American society and his ultimate rejection of the "man of sense" persona.

He did continue for a time to pose in white man's clothes, however, though the outfit that he wears in these photos is only a temporary costume meant for special ceremonial occasions, as evidenced by the highly starched striped dickey, or detachable shirtfront.[5] It is not known whether Red Cloud owned this lavish outfit or whose idea it was for him to wear it, but his posing in these clothes does point to the complicated nature of his public persona during this difficult period in Oglala affairs.

Like many commercial photographers of the time, Trager aggressively marketed cabinet-card views of celebrated Plains Indians to local residents and travelers who were passing through Nebraska. The expansion of railroad lines across the Great Plains and a growing interest in the welfare of Native cultures was leading to increased contact between Euro-Americans and the Lakotas. With the opening of the Badlands and Yellowstone National Park as tourist destinations, many easterners combined sojourns at notable natural wonders with visits to Native communities. The Omaha and Winnebago reservations in eastern Nebraska were especially attractive to transcontinental passengers, given their proximity to established accommodations and railroad stations, not to mention their relative peace and prosperity.

Pine Ridge, by contrast, remained off the beaten track, but those who did visit often found that the reality of Lakota life

49. Red Cloud, 1890 or 1891. Photograph by George Trager. Western History Collection, Denver Public Library, Denver CO (X-31326).

was a far cry from the images being circulated in the East. As one traveler wrote, "All Indian land is constantly improving in quality in the estimation of white men who want the reservations opened, but I have seen very few who knew much about it, in fact, or had ever taken the trouble to examine any of it carefully. The proportion of arable land to the whole extent of these two reservations (Pine Ridge and Rosebud) is very small, not more, I think, than one-eighth of the whole. . . . The remainder is fit only for pasturage, and much of it is as barren and useless as the central desolation of Sahara."[6]

Pine Ridge Agency, South Dakota, 1890–91

The portrait showing Red Cloud in a wide-brimmed hat (figure 49) was taken at the height of interest in the Ghost Dance. Though his son Jack embraced this movement, Red Cloud was skeptical of the Ghost Dance and remained uncharacteristically silent during the disturbances that accompanied its rise in popularity. Charles Eastman (Ohiyesa), an eastern-educated doctor and member of the Santee tribe who came to work as a government doctor at Pine Ridge in 1890, remembered that Red Cloud "would come to council, but said little or nothing. No one knew exactly where he stood, but it seemed that he was broken in spirit as in body and convinced of the hopelessness of his people's cause."[7]

Given his long history of conflict with American authorities, though, non-Natives were suspicious of Red Cloud's apparent lack of approval of the Ghost Dance. Dr. Daniel Royer, the newly installed agent to the Oglalas, was one such individual. On October 30, 1890, he wrote

to Commissioner of Indian Affairs Robert V. Belt, "While Red Cloud is not a prominent man in the dance, he is quietly encouraging his people to keep it going."[8]

Red Cloud's own words from this period, however, contradict Royer's assessment. In a December 10, 1890, letter to his friend Thomas A. Bland, he claimed not to be a part of the Ghost Dance and tried to dispel the idea that war was imminent. The following is an excerpt from that letter:

You know I am the same all the time, I am true and have not changed. I am the constant friend of the whites, and all that has been said about my preparing my people for war is false and a lie, for they do not desire or intend to go on the war-path. The soldiers are here and treat us all very well; we have no fault to find with them. My people (the Ogallalas) are all here now; they came at the request of the Military. Since they all arrived we have had several open councils among my people only, which resulted in an unanimous agreement to stop the Ghost Dance, and so far as the dance is concerned I can truly say that I never had anything to do with or encourage it, never having seen one. . . . My country is divided into four districts. In each of them we have schools and churches. All my people have houses which they built themselves like white men, and it is unreasonable to suppose such people as mine established as they are here, would go to war with the U.S. Government to whom they have to look for the very necessities of life to say nothing of the fact that my country is surrounded by railroads and white farmers and towns; it must be apparent that there is no room for us to go to war.[9]

Nevertheless, Indian Bureau authorities in the East worried about how to respond to the growing tension. One artist at the *New York World* drew a cartoon (figure 50) suggesting a farcical solution to the "Indian troubles." Published on the paper's front page on November 30, 1890, it played upon the myth of Native Americans' fear of the camera as an instrument that supposedly stole people's souls.

Pine Ridge Agency, South Dakota, January 1891

December 1890 was a tragic month in Lakota tribal history. Another harsh winter brought hunger and suffering to a population already weakened by disease and disillusionment. Though it was creating serious intratribal divisions, the Ghost Dance continued to attract many Lakota men with its promise of a return to the days before the white man's arrival. In the meantime, newly arrived settlers from the East feared that an uprising was likely and called on the U.S. military to protect them.

Despite his advanced age, Sitting Bull, whose military exploits more than a decade before had captured the American public's attention, once again became the focus of white suspicion. Government officials ordered his arrest, and Indian police showed up at his home on the morning of December 15; a fight ensued, and in the midst of the confusion, Sitting Bull was shot dead.

Further human tragedy awaited the Lakotas two weeks later. On the banks of Wounded Knee creek, twenty-five miles northeast of Pine Ridge agency, a force of 500 American soldiers confronted 350 Lakotas, two-thirds of whom were women and children. Although they were in fact only looking for sustenance and refuge from the bitter cold, the authori-

ties – recognizing some members of this Native band as Ghost Dancers – feared a military attack, and orders were given to disarm those carrying guns. Fighting broke out, and several hours later eighty-four men and sixty-two women and children lay dead. The next day, a blizzard blanketed the earth with snow.

Reports of these hostilities soon reached the American public. For the next month, newspapers across the nation told and retold this tragic event. Many writers blamed the Lakotas for precipitating the actions at Wounded Knee, describing them as "treacherous," "hateful," and "insane" and calling for stricter measures to protect Euro-American settlers. One voice countering these charges was that of George Bird Grinnell, an important naturalist and ethnologist who edited the popular conservation magazine *Forest and Stream*. Having accompanied Custer's 1874 expedition into the Black Hills, Grinnell was familiar with the troubles that the Lakotas faced. In an editorial in the *New York Tribune* he blamed the "massacre of the Indians" on "the bad judgment of the [U.S.] officer in command. . . . It was an act of insanity to attempt forcibly to disarm these surrendering Indians, and anyone familiar with the nature and modes of thinking of the Indian could certainly have predicted that such an attempt would result in desperate fighting."[10] As well reasoned as Grinnell's argument was, few within Euro-American society accepted his interpretation. Instead, age-old stereotypes of Native peoples were resurrected to explain and legitimize what had happened.

In the following weeks, despite the severe weather, five local photographers traveled to Wounded Knee to record the

50. "To Settle the Indian Troubles."
New York World, November 30, 1890.
General Research Division, New
York Public Library, Astor, Lenox,
and Tilden Foundations.

51. Red Cloud and others at Wounded Knee, 1891. Photograph by Clarence G. Morledge. Western History Collection, Denver Public Library, Denver CO (X-31313).

52. *Left to right:* Red Cloud, Major John Burke, Rocky Bear, 1891. Photograph by Clarence G. Morledge. Nebraska State Historical Society, Lincoln (RG2845:119-49).

aftermath.[11] Hoping to sell views to an American public engrossed by this conflict, the photographers spent several weeks on the former battlefield. Over the following months the resulting images became important to those attempting to explain the event.

Red Cloud was not present at Wounded Knee on the day of the fighting. Several days earlier, Two Strike, one of the Ghost Dance leaders, and others – tired of Red Cloud's efforts at negotiating a settlement – had abducted him and led him to a hideout known as the Stronghold. Ten days after the conflict, Red Cloud escaped back to Pine Ridge, where he explained to officials that he had been trying unsuccessfully to persuade the last of the "hostiles" to surrender. Not until January 15 did Two Strike, Kicking Bear, and the remainder of the Ghost Dancers come in and hand over their arms to military authorities, thereby bringing this chapter of the episode to an end.[12]

One of the five photographers at Wounded Knee was Clarence G. Morledge, who took a picture (figure 51) of the camp where the U.S. Army's First Infantry had been stationed. Soldiers are in the midst of breaking down and packing up their tents, watched by a group of Native individuals. In the foreground the image of Red Cloud facing Morledge's camera captures his liminal status during this period, reduced from participant to observer in tribal affairs.

Another Morledge photograph shows Red Cloud and his fellow tribesman Rocky Bear on either side of Major John Burke, the general manager of Buffalo Bill's Wild West Show (figure 52). Wearing goggles to protect his sensitive eyes, dressed in a dark jacket and moccasins,

and standing with little expression before an agency building at Pine Ridge, Red Cloud seems neither the warrior of repute nor the tribal diplomat but rather an aging reservation dweller. Rocky Bear, returning from a tour of Europe with the Wild West Show, had served as an intermediary between the Ghost Dancers and military authorities during this crisis, attempting with Red Cloud and others to avert an armed conflict.

He and many individuals associated with the Wild West Show, including not only Major Burke but William "Buffalo Bill" Cody himself, were at Pine Ridge both before and after the hostilities of December 29. A month earlier, General Nelson Miles, the commander of U.S. military forces in the West, had chosen Cody to arrest Sitting Bull. Because the Hunkpapa leader had spent the summer of 1885 performing with the Wild West Show, Miles believed that Cody's friendship with Sitting Bull would enable him to do the job peacefully. Not long thereafter, though, President Benjamin Harrison rescinded the order, following the vehement protest of Major James McLaughlin, the agent overseeing Sitting Bull's Hunkpapas; McLaughlin wanted to oversee the arrest himself. Hence, Cody remained at the periphery of the action.

He reemerged after the surrender and subsequent imprisonment of Kicking Bear and his followers. Cody understood the potential drawing power of such a group in his show and worked to have authorities place them in his custody. It took several months of negotiations, but he did secure the release of Kicking Bear and twenty-two of his followers who had been imprisoned at Fort Sheridan, Illinois; it was for this reason that Major

53. Chief Red Cloud's home, Pine Ridge, South Dakota, 1891. Photograph by Clarence G. Morledge. Kansas State Historical Society, Topeka.

54. Red Cloud (*standing, center*), Major John Burke (*kneeling, center*), and others, 1891. Photograph by Clarence G. Morledge. Western History Collection, Denver Public Library, Denver CO (X-31460).

Burke was on the reservation at the time. (Cody had wanted Red Cloud to join the group, too, but the old chief turned him down.) Together with Cody's theatrical troupe, these Wounded Knee survivors spent the next year touring Europe.

In 1879, American authorities had built a two-story wooden house for Red Cloud at Pine Ridge. They hoped that new dwellings would push him and other Oglalas toward "civilization" and a more accommodationist position with government officials.

Continuing his photographic tour of the reservation in 1891, Morledge arranged to take several photographs of Red Cloud outside this house. In one of these (figure 53), Red Cloud stands beside his flagpole with his wife, Pretty Owl, and Major Burke; an unidentified person stands about six feet away. The cooperation that Red Cloud exhibited not only with Major Burke but also with photographers such as Morledge, Trager, and later John H. Grabill during their visits to Pine Ridge suggests his desire to normalize U.S.-Oglala relations in the aftermath of the tragedy at Wounded Knee.

For some time, Red Cloud had felt an urgent need to address the great divide that existed between the two nations. Just before Wounded Knee he had spoken despondently about the state of affairs involving the Oglalas and the management of their reservation. In an interview with Francis M. Craft, a Catholic missionary who was subsequently wounded during the conflict, Red Cloud stressed the corruption and incompetence of prior agents and the pressing need to overhaul the entire system. Agents "take care of themselves and not of us," and "it is very hard to deal with the government only

through them," he exclaimed. "The Indian Department has almost destroyed us. Save us from it. Let the army take charge of us. We know it can help us. Let it manage our affairs in its own ways."[13] Twelve years earlier, Red Cloud had rejected the idea of having the military manage the reservation system. His change of opinion indicates his exasperation with the current state of affairs.

Red Cloud hung a Morledge photograph from this series in his bedroom (see figure 2), probably because it presented a flattering portrait of him and his wife outside their comfortable home. In truth, however, conditions on the reservation – not to mention U.S.-Oglala relations – were far from good. Red Cloud may have displayed this particular portrait to help ease his troubled mind.

Pine Ridge Agency, South Dakota, Spring 1891

Amid a large crowd of Native Americans and whites, Red Cloud and Major Burke posed again before the photographer's camera (figure 54). Red Cloud stands in the middle of this group, while Burke kneels on one knee beside him; each is holding on to an unidentifiable book, perhaps symbolizing some union or agreement. In light of the recent events at Pine Ridge, it is ironic that Burke assumes a deferential posture before the standing figure of Red Cloud. As with the image that the old chief hung in his home, photographic reality did not accurately reflect the actual events unfolding on the reservation.

Morledge made this particular photograph during the spring of 1891. Snow is no longer on the ground, one indication

Chief Red Clouts Home
Pine Ridge S.D.

55. "Red Cloud and American Horse – The Two Most Noted Chiefs Now Living," 1891. Photograph by John H. Grabill. Library of Congress, Washington DC.

that it was taken at a later date than his earlier portraits of Red Cloud. To assemble a large and diverse group of photographs for marketing under his newly established American Viewing Company label, Morledge remained at Pine Ridge until summer. It was during this time that he took several indoor views of Red Cloud's home (see figure 2). Red Cloud's willingness to allow Morledge to photograph the interior at least twice suggests the friendly relationship that they shared. It also points to Red Cloud's larger desire to be figured in the photographic record that Morledge and others were assembling.

Pine Ridge Agency, South Dakota, Spring 1891

John H. Grabill, a commercial photographer from Deadwood, South Dakota, dedicated several seasons to recording Native American life on the northern Plains. Not long after the conflict at Wounded Knee, he too traveled to Pine Ridge to procure images of the battle's aftermath. The highlight of this visit was the opportunity to photograph Red Cloud and American Horse together (figure 55). The significance that Grabill assigned to their meeting is reflected in the title he gave the resulting image, "Red Cloud and American Horse – The Two Most Noted Chiefs Now Living." This caption points not so subtly to the tragic events of the previous winter.

In February 1891, General Miles had invited an Oglala delegation, led by Young Man Afraid of His Horses and American Horse, to Washington to discuss the events of the preceding two months and to speak about the future of U.S.-Oglala

affairs. Red Cloud, much to his consternation, was denied permission to accompany this delegation by Secretary of the Interior John W. Noble, partially because Red Cloud had disobeyed his order to remain at home two years earlier. In an attempt to circumvent Noble's decision, Red Cloud wrote his old friend Othniel Marsh in New Haven to seek help in lining up permission and funds to travel east. Ultimately, though, Marsh was unable to accomplish what Red Cloud wanted, and the embittered chief was left out of the proceedings.[14]

Though Red Cloud remained at odds with government officials during this period, he and American Horse reconciled their political differences and ended their year-long personal feud. With a tipi as background, Grabill photographed them shaking hands, a symbol of their reunion. Ever mindful of his appearance before the camera, Red Cloud wears a full headdress for the occasion and holds a blanket over his arm, perhaps a gift either to or from American Horse. As he had done repeatedly for twenty years, Red Cloud publicized an event in his life, this renewal of friendship, before the white man's camera.

Unknown Location, 1890s

Following Wounded Knee, an event that many Euro-Americans came to understand as the "end of the Indian wars," the Lakotas entered a period of less active resistance. Although their leaders, including Red Cloud, continued to speak out about problems on the reservation, most Native communities worked to recover from the trauma of Wounded Knee and to adjust to living on a reservation whose size had been cut almost by half in the preceding two years. Some pro-Indian reformers within Euro-American society expressed concern about the difficult position in which the Lakotas found themselves in the wake of Wounded Knee but, as time passed, paid less and less attention. At least for the time being, most non-Natives wanted simply to forget about Wounded Knee and the Lakotas' plight.

One sign of their declining interest was that the commercial trade in Native American photographs largely dried up. Although images of Wounded Knee sold well in the months directly after the event itself, for several years thereafter, few photographers sought out Native subjects. Only once in the next half-decade did Red Cloud sit for his portrait, this time with his son Jack and two friends: the Oglala chief called Knife and the trader-interpreter Baptiste Garnier (figure 56). Rather than being aimed at a mass market, this photograph was most likely commissioned as a personal memento.

Like his father, Jack Red Cloud also posed for the camera many times, but this is the earliest photograph in which father and son are pictured together. Jack, born in 1852, grew up in the shadow of his father. During both the Great Sioux War and the hostilities surrounding the Ghost Dance, he followed the path of those who chose to fight the American military. Though Red Cloud remained at the periphery of both conflicts, he supported his son's resistance.

In the events leading up to the battle at Wounded Knee, Jack was particularly outspoken in his criticism of American Horse's acquiescence to U.S. authorities. At one heated moment in this conflict, according to the Pine Ridge doctor Charles Eastman, he confronted American Horse,

thrust a revolver into his face, and shouted, "It is you and your kind who have brought us to this pass!"[15] American Horse walked away, and a fight was avoided.

In addition to Jack, Red Cloud and Pretty Owl raised five daughters. On no occasion, however, did Red Cloud ever pose with his daughters – a sign not so much of his feelings toward them as of the conventions of the photographic trade.

Studio of Charles Bell, Washington DC, May 1897

In the spring of 1897, at the age of seventy-six, Red Cloud made his tenth and final trip to Washington. He and American Horse led an Oglala delegation that went east to present a long list of grievances to President William McKinley and Indian Bureau officials. These issues included continuing trouble with Pine Ridge Agent William H. Clapp and other non-Natives working on the reservation, especially the superintendent of the reservation school. This man's strict manner and the harsh discipline that he and his staff handed out to students were upsetting to Native families. In a letter to the commissioner of Indian affairs, which Red Cloud endorsed, Oglala leaders "asked that a more humane and experienced man be appointed to take control of the boarding school, which is to have in the future such potent influence either for good or evil in the formation of the character of our youth."[16]

Before the Senate Committee on Indian Affairs, Red Cloud also reasserted his disdain for the land allotment system. Explaining that the reservation lands on

56. Clockwise from top left: Chief Knife, Jack Red Cloud, Baptiste Garnier, Red Cloud. Photographer unknown. Courtesy of South Dakota State Historical Society – State Archives, Pierre.

57. *Left to right:* George Sword, American Horse, Charles P. Jordan, Red Cloud, Charles Eastman, 1897. Studio of Charles Bell. National Anthropological Archives, Smithsonian Institution, Washington DC (52838).

which the Oglalas lived were unsuited for agricultural production, he asked that "the good men of Congress . . . make an effort to assist us in keeping the reservation common to us all." South Dakota Senator Richard F. Pettigrew, though, the committee chair, refused to revisit this subject and thereafter steered Red Cloud's testimony to less controversial matters.

Cognizant of the significance of this moment, Red Cloud used the occasion also to say goodbye to his diplomatic counterparts and to impress upon them the importance of cooperation in the future: "My friend [Senator Pettigrew], you know that I am getting old and blind, and I am not fit to go anywhere. Really, it is a great effort for me to come here, but I wanted to come and grasp my friends' hands and make my last appeal to them to stick to their promises, and to grant what we have to ask. It is reasonable."[17]

Three days later, when the delegation met briefly with the new president, Red Cloud was unable to attend because he was not feeling well.[18] And, as so often in the past, little came of these discussions.

Before leaving Washington, Red Cloud was strong enough to return to the photographic studio of Charles Bell (though Bell had died four years earlier, his family continued to run the business under his name until 1909). There, sitting beside American Horse and clutching his cane, Red Cloud posed again for a family that he had first met in 1880. Standing behind him are, from left to right, George Sword, Charles P. Jordan, and Charles Eastman (figure 57). As befits their situation, all five men wear suits and ties. Red Cloud's acknowledgment to Pettigrew that he was beginning to lose his eyesight explains why he wears dark goggles in this and other photographs from his later years.

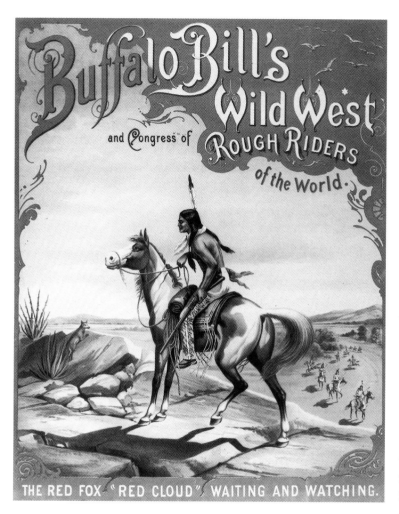

THE RED FOX "RED CLOUD" WAITING AND WATCHING.

58. "The Red Fox 'Red Cloud' Waiting and Watching," 1893. August Hoen & Company. Buffalo Bill Historical Society, Cody WY (1.69.443).

59. *Left to right:* Red Cloud, William "Buffalo Bill" Cody, American Horse, 1897. Photograph by David Barry. Western History Collection, Denver Public Library, Denver CO (B-725).

Madison Square Garden, New York City, May 1897

Before returning home, the party traveled to New York City, where they met the famed showman William "Buffalo Bill" Cody. Having served as an army scout and a buffalo hunter on the Great Plains during his youth, Cody had transformed these experiences into a theatrical career that made him one of the most well-known figures of his day both in the United States and abroad.

With its concentration on such acts as trick riding and shooting, his Wild West Show, then performing in New York, presented a highly romanticized rendition of life in the American West. Cody's decision in 1885 to recruit Native Americans for the show excited audiences but often left the Native performers with ambivalent feelings about the enterprise. Cody had commissioned a poster of Red Cloud in 1893 (figure 58), and he asked Red Cloud repeatedly to tour with the show. He went so far as to offer the chief $150 per month plus all expenses.[19] But although Sitting Bull and many other Lakota leaders signed up, Red Cloud never accepted the invitation.

On this occasion, however, he and American Horse did agree to sit for a series of publicity portraits at Madison Square Garden with Cody, who embraced the chance to be photographed alongside the two delegation leaders. In figure 59, Buffalo Bill stands between Red Cloud and American Horse. Both chiefs wear warbonnets and other Native paraphernalia to heighten the Old West aura.

For two other views, the three men pose on horseback; ever the entertainer, Cody is attempting to play up the chiefs'

60. Red Cloud on horseback (*left*) with William "Buffalo Bill" Cody and American Horse, 1897. Photograph by David Barry. Western History Collection, Denver Public Library, Denver CO (B-724).

61. Red Cloud on horseback (*left*) with William "Buffalo Bill" Cody and American Horse, 1897. Photograph by David Barry. Western History Collection, Denver Public Library, Denver CO (B-719).

storied past. Red Cloud's cane indicates the contrived nature of this scene, however, and he again wears the dark goggles (figure 60).

For a second photograph on horseback, Red Cloud and Cody shake hands (figure 61). Though many Native Americans criticized Cody and the Wild West Show for perpetuating racist stereotypes, and though Red Cloud never joined the show, he seems ready enough to shake hands with Buffalo Bill.

David Frances Barry was the photographer for the Madison Square Garden series. Raised in Wisconsin, he had operated several photographic studios in the Mid-west before relocating to New York City in January 1897. His studio was around the corner from the Garden, a location from which Barry believed he could develop a successful business. He had photographed Native Americans before and was eager to establish a relationship with Cody's Wild West Show. A year later, though, Barry returned to Wisconsin, an indication that his New York venture was not the boon he had expected.[20]

Barry also created a highly romanticized portrait of Red Cloud, carefully removing both the cane and the dark goggles (figure 62). Despite Red Cloud's age, the resulting image represents the Oglala chief as a heroic figure from another era: namely, the "Old West," that period at midcentury when Native warriors and American military forces transformed the Great Plains into one large battleground. Like the photograph itself, this version of western history was carefully constructed to meet certain cultural agendas. For one, it helped to legitimate the subjugation of Native Americans and the occupation of their homelands. In addition, given profound changes in the workplace and in the ethnic makeup of American society, it served to mask fin-de-siècle crises in American masculinity and immigration policy.[21] Embracing a figure like Red Cloud – or buying a photograph of him – allowed one to participate vicariously in a past that seemed both simpler and more robust.

62. Red Cloud, 1897. Photograph by David Barry. National Anthropological Archives, Smithsonian Institution, Washington DC (3237-C).

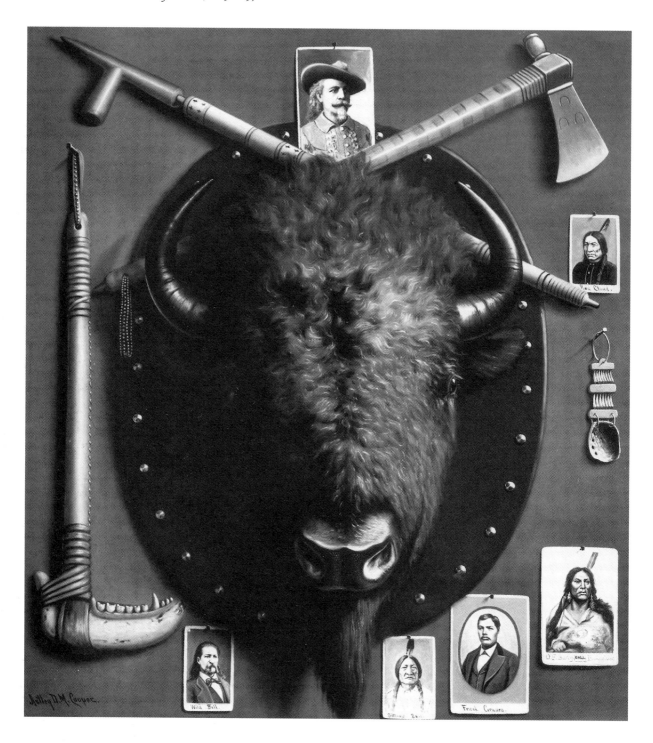

63. *The Buffalo Head*, 1890s. Painting by Astley D. M. Cooper. Buffalo Bill Historical Center, Cody WY (4.64).

64. *Left to right:* Red Cloud, John Burke, American Horse, 1897. Photograph by David Barry. Western History Collection, Denver Public Library, Denver CO (B-730).

As the success of the Wild West Show reveals, many Euro-Americans cultivated an interest in the myth of the "Old West" at the end of the century. Painted in the same period as Barry's photograph, Astley D. M. Cooper's trompe l'oeil still life *The Buffalo Head* (figure 63) reveals a similar fascination. Surrounding the mounted buffalo head are a collection of "traditional" Native American artifacts and six cabinet-card photographs of individuals whose lives were an intimate part of this bygone era. Positioned grandly at the top of the canvas is a photograph of William Cody. To his right and slightly lower, Cooper has painted a photograph of Red

Cloud, based loosely on a photograph taken two decades earlier (figure 24). Cooper's decision to include this image speaks both to Euro-American society's understanding of Red Cloud as a dramatic character from the distant past and to photography's ability to recall those memories.

Two photographs in Barry's series picture Red Cloud and American Horse with two of Cody's leading partners. In one (figure 64), John Burke, the general manager of the Wild West Show, poses with the two Oglala leaders as he had with Red Cloud at Pine Ridge in the aftermath of Wounded Knee.

65. *Left to right*: Red Cloud, Nate Salsbury, American Horse, 1897. Photograph by David Barry. Western History Collection, Denver Public Library, Denver CO (B-733).

In the program for the 1886 season, Burke articulated best the goals of the Wild West Show:

It is the aim of the management of Buffalo Bill's Wild West to do more than present an exacting and realistic entertainment for the public amusement. The object is to PICTURE TO THE EYE, *by aid of historical characters and living animals, a series of animated scenes and episodes, which had their existence in fact, of the wonderful pioneer and frontier life of the Wild West of America. Beginning with the Primeval Forest, peopled by the Indian and Wild Beasts only, the story of the gradual civilization of a vast continent is depicted. The hard-*

ships, daring, and frontier skill of the participants being a guarantee of the faithful reproduction of scenes and incidents in which they had actual experience. The central figure in these pictures is that of THE HON. W. F. CODY *(Buffalo Bill), to whose sagacity, skill, energy, and courage . . . the settlers of the West owe so much for the reclamation of the prairie from the savage Indian and wild animals, who so long opposed the march of civilization.*[22]

At the century's end, the public flocked to photographs of Native Americans and the Wild West Show for similar reasons. Both promised to present a transparent window into a culture that most non-Na-

66. Red Cloud, Annie Oakley, American Horse (*left to right, front row, center*), and others, 1897. Photograph by David Barry. Western History Collection, Denver Public Library, Denver CO (B-731).

tives believed was fast disappearing. Yet such visual amusements were ultimately able to construct only a fictitious representation of their subjects.

Nate Salsbury, one of the original founders of the Wild West Show, replaces Burke in the second portrait (figure 65). In 1882 he had organized a grand equestrian exhibition starring Cody. A veteran showman who had learned much about the entertainment business with his touring musical company, "Salsbury's Troubadours," he helped to transform the Wild West Show into a financial bonanza. In 1897 he continued to serve as one of Cody's principal partners and

therefore was given an opportunity to pose between Red Cloud and American Horse, both of whom continued to sit patiently before Barry's camera.

As so much of the Wild West Show was built around fantasy, the presence of these two Oglala chiefs must have helped to legitimate, if only for a short while, the show's supposed realism. Perhaps that is why Barry completed at least a dozen photographs at this time.

In figure 66, Red Cloud and American Horse join a large part of the cast, including Annie Oakley, the famed female sharpshooter, who sits between the two Oglala leaders. It is perhaps significant

that Red Cloud has taken off his headdress for this photograph. Wearing feathers in one's hair was a symbol of distinguished conduct among the Lakotas and
often indicated one's rank within society.
Only those who had attained a certain
status were traditionally permitted to
wear a feather warbonnet, but because
show managers routinely distributed
warbonnets to Native participants, their
larger cultural significance was rapidly
losing its meaning.

Red Cloud's decision to remove his
headdress may suggest his disillusionment with the kind of popular entertainment in which so many of the Native
males were decked out in warbonnnets.
Though wearing feathers alongside Cody,
American Horse, and other important
figures may not have offended Red Cloud
– indeed, it might have seemed altogether
appropriate to wear such formal dress
when interacting with distinguished individuals – perhaps he thought the
warbonnet's real significance was too
great for such casual treatment. Native
symbols retained their significance to Red
Cloud, and though he might agree to
meet and pose alongside Cody and others
from his Wild West Show, he was reluctant to allow Native traditions to be
wholly appropriated by the dominant
culture.

Besides the attention, it is unclear
what Red Cloud and American Horse received for participating in this extended
photographic session. Perhaps they were
paid; given his success, Cody was able to
compensate the individuals in his troupe
quite well, including the Native American performers. Though their facial expressions suggest a sense of boredom
with the proceedings, perhaps they en-

joyed the show. As Burke had declared,
Cody sought to resurrect the old frontier
days, and Red Cloud, now a frail old man,
may have relished the opportunity to remember fondly the triumphs of his
youth. At the least, these photographs reveal that Cody and others revered him.

5. The Icon, 1898–1909

Though his 1897 trip to Washington was his last diplomatic excursion, Red Cloud remained involved in tribal affairs during the remaining twelve years of his life. Despite failing eyesight, he continued to travel and regularly made himself available to the many photographers who sought him out. Indeed, Red Cloud sat for more portraits during this period than at any other time in his career – partially because the development of new photographic technologies had made the medium cheaper and easier to use. More important, though, Red Cloud had attained iconic status within American society. Well known as a warrior and then a tribal diplomat, he increasingly came to represent the now mythic "Old West." At the same time, these later photographs reveal that Red Cloud's own sense of himself changed during this period. Less active as an Oglala leader, he favored memories of the past and personal relationships to a greater degree than the political issues that still troubled his tribe. In addition, he seems to have acceded to the concept of himself as "Indian" icon.

Studio of Frank Rinehart, Omaha, Nebraska, August 1898

Though old age was slowing Red Cloud down, he traveled to Omaha, Nebraska, for the Trans-Mississippi and International Exposition in August 1898. Inspired by the World's Columbian Exposition five years earlier in Chicago, this world's fair showcased the "progress" of the American West at the century's end. In addition to agricultural and manufacturing displays, officials organized special exhibits that drew attention to the exceptionalism of the West. Included among these attractions was the "Indian Encampment," where more than five hundred Native Americans from twenty tribes participated in various demonstrations.[1] Such celebrated chiefs as Red Cloud, American Horse, Chief Joseph, and Geronimo all accepted invitations to come to Omaha.

Edward Rosewater, a local newspaper editor, first conceived the idea of a pan-Indian exhibition, believing that such a display would be both educational and a big ticket-seller. Because he was unfamiliar with Native cultures and reservation politics, Rosewater recruited a Bureau of American Ethnology anthropologist, James Mooney, to organize the gathering. The explanatory circular that Mooney distributed to reservation agents in the months prior to the Indian Encampment provides a glimpse into his vision of this attraction.

It is the purpose of the proposed encampment or congress to make an extensive exhibit illustrative of the mode of life, native industries, and ethnic traits of as many aboriginal American tribes as possible. To that end it is proposed to bring together selected families or groups from all the principal tribes, and camp them in tepees, wigwams, hogans, etc., on the exposition grounds, and there permit them to conduct their domestic affairs as they do at home, and make and sell their wares for their own profit. It is desired that the encampment should be as thoroughly aboriginal in every respect as practicable, and that the primitive traits and characteristics of the several tribes should be distinctly set forth. This point should be constantly kept in view in the selection of the Indians and in the collection of materials. They should bring their native dress, if possible. They should also bring their native domiciles or the materials with which to make them. They should also bring the necessary articles with which to furnish and decorate their tepee or other domiciles.[2]

Not unlike the many photographers who sought out nostalgic images of a mythic Native American past, the exhibit organizers were unconcerned about the reality of contemporary tribal life. Instead, only whatever was "thoroughly aboriginal" was deemed suitable for display. Hence, though earlier photographs of Red Cloud had emphasized his capacity for acculturation, Frank Rinehart's profile portrait of the old chief (figure 67), like the display of which he was a part, aimed to erase all traces of his long-standing relationship with Euro-American society.

Though Mooney envisioned the exhibit as a serious ethnographic project, the Indian Encampment was ultimately transformed into a popular spectacle, intended to entertain rather than to educate visitors. On the one day during the summer when the exposition's managers highlighted this gathering of Native peoples, they proposed that the central activity of "Indian Day" be a sham battle between a group of Native Americans and a local fraternal organization, the Improved Order of the Red Men. Rosewater's newspaper praised the idea and editorialized that "it was fit that this reunion should be held here since encamped on the grounds were perhaps the last remnants of those aborigines whose better rites and qualities it was the noble purpose of the Improved Order of the Red Men to perpetuate. Here was a great lesson for the order – the representatives of the old life on the Plains and in the wilderness and the luxury and art and achievement of the civilization that had succeeded."[3]

Citing logistical problems, however, the Red Men backed out at the last moment, and the mock battle was placed under the direction of managers from the Wild West Show. The newspaper reported that the Native Americans defeated their "civilized" foes in a rout and that they enjoyed themselves immensely.[4] Afterward, all the participants paraded past the reviewing stand and saluted President William McKinley and General Nelson A. Miles, both present for the day's activities.[5]

This fair, like the Wild West Show itself, only furthered the popular belief that though they were victorious in the exposition's arena, Native Americans were verging on cultural extinction. Red Cloud's aged countenance seemed to bear out that idea. In demand because he added a semblance of authenticity to the ersatz performances, he found himself once again being used by the non-Native community.

Not surprisingly, the exposition's official photographer, Frank Rinehart, arranged a studio session with the chief. Figure 68 is one of three photographs that he took at the time, and shows off most completely the beaded shirt and blanket that Red Cloud wore, and the pipe and beaded pipe bag that he held. Interestingly, his shirt is the work of a Crow artist, and several other members of the Lakota delegation wore the same shirt for their portraits.[6] It is therefore probable that Rinehart lent it to the chief in his concern to create portraits that figured his subjects as distinctly "Indian." Red Cloud's willingness to wear articles of clothing that did not belong to him suggests how accommodating he was on this occasion.

Not only was Rinehart compiling a series of Native American views that he hoped to market to the public, but the Bureau of American Ethnology was also interested in acquiring a set of photographic portraits of those Native Americans who had traveled to Omaha; it made available a special fund to help underwrite the project. Mooney encouraged Rinehart and his assistant, Adolf Muhr, to follow a "systematic plan" so that the government agency might take home "bust, profile, and full length" portraits of representative leaders.[7] By the exposition's end, Rinehart had completed almost two hundred portraits of seventy different Native Americans.[8]

Though fairgoers might have concluded that Red Cloud's days of protest and resistance were long over, he remained in fact a frequent critic of the federal government and the administration that oversaw the reservation system. Earlier in 1898, for example, he had opposed –

68. Red Cloud, 1898. Photograph by Frank Rinehart. National Anthropological Archives, Smithsonian Institution, Washington DC (3238-0).

albeit unsuccessfully – the appropriation of federal monies to construct a sixty-mile-long fence along the northern boundary of the Oglala reservation. Meant to keep out cattle that non-Native ranchers were raising in the area, the fence represented to Red Cloud a tremendous waste of time and money. Likewise, as he articulated in a letter to the commissioner of Indian affairs, he worried that funds granted to the Lakotas under the 1889 land agreement with the federal government would be used to pay for something that the Oglalas did not want.[9] Because of the long history of government abuse and corruption toward his people, Red Cloud remained wary of any such intrusion.

In addition to opposing the fence, he continued to reject the policy of land allotment outlined in the Dawes Act of 1887. Many of his fellow Oglalas adopted the "progressive" agenda that Euro-American reformers advocated, but Red Cloud maintained his stubborn opposition to many of its tenets.

Yet at the same time, he was willing to participate in studio sessions that might easily be construed as shameless exploitation on the part of the photographer. As sensitive to slights against both himself and his people as he was, Red Cloud apparently saw these occasions in a different light: photography, a vital means for self-expression, brought him needed attention and allowed him to remain in the public spotlight (figure 69). In addition, photographers often paid him to pose, and given the impoverished conditions on the reservation, this money was always welcome.

69. Red Cloud, 1898. Photograph by Frank Rinehart. National Anthropological Archives, Smithsonian Institution, Washington DC (3238-P).

70. "Chief Red Cloud – Age 77, Sioux," 1898. Photograph by Jesse H. Bratley. Library of Congress, Washington DC.

Pine Ridge Agency, South Dakota, 1898

Because Red Cloud traveled less and less frequently during the last decade of his life, commercial photographers, understanding the lasting marketability of his name, often visited him at Pine Ridge. As the success of Buffalo Bill's Wild West Show and the Omaha exposition illustrated, non-Native audiences were enthralled by Native American individuals whose lives had been wrapped up in the storied military conflicts on the Great Plains. Such narratives functioned as a way for Euro-Americans to reconcile tensions caused by the rapidly changing world around them. With thousands of new immigrants arriving in America and industrialization reshaping the contours of society, many turned to the "Old West" not only as an escape but as a means to understand better their own place in this world.

As a group, the late photographs reflect American society's nostalgia toward Red Cloud and Native Americans in general. Faced with new "problems" both from overseas and at home, many Americans now understood the once heated "Indian problem" as a figment of the historical past. Confined to reservations, Native peoples were now subject to the mythologizing gaze of the dominant culture. The many photographers who passed through Pine Ridge failed to see or to document the social and political problems that gripped the Oglalas and other Native American tribes.

Jesse H. Bratley was one such photographer who traveled and, having befriended Red Cloud, took at least seven photographs of the old chief. In one of these (figure 70), Red Cloud stands only a few feet from the camera. He holds a pipe and pipe bag and wears a leather shirt with beaded figures depicting mounted horsemen.

In addition to his work as a photographer, Bratley also taught at various Native American schools. A strong believer in the campaign to "civilize the Indian," he had began teaching in 1895 at the Lower Cut Meat Creek Indian Day School on the nearby Rosebud reservation. There he directed classes in such vocational skills as farming, irrigation, carpentry, and blacksmithing. Then, following a four-year tenure, he moved on to work among the Native peoples in Oklahoma.[10] During his time at Rosebud, however, he traveled widely to photograph many of the famous old Lakota chiefs who lived in the region.

No. 171.
COPYRIGHT. 1898.
By J. H. BRATLEY.
Chief Red Cloud. Age 73.
Sioux.

Though a champion of "civilization,"
Bratley played up Red Cloud's "Indianness." He probably asked the chief to as-
sume the pose in figure 71, for Lakotas
did not smoke on such occasions, nor did
they hold the pipe as Red Cloud does
here. Because pipe smoking was regarded
as a traditional Native custom, this sort
of pose only reinforced stereotypical ideas
about Lakota culture.

71. Red Cloud, 1898. Photograph
by Jesse H. Bratley. National Anthropological Archives, Smithsonian Institution, Washington DC
(53317-A).

A close-up view (figure 72) highlights Red Cloud's aged face and the beaded figures on his leather shirt. In one hand, he holds his cane.

72. Red Cloud, 1898. Photograph by Jesse H. Bratley. Handbook of the North American Indians Project, Breckenridge Collection, Smithsonian Institution, Washington DC.

Bratley tried to market these views, even going so far as to copyright many of his portraits, but does not seem to have had great success in this venture. In subsequent years, Frank Rinehart obtained Bratley's negatives and used them to supplement his own important collection of Native American portraits. Before issuing Bratley's photographs under his own name, though, Rinehart made some significant alterations to the prints. As figure 73 indicates, he painted in a pipe where the cane had been, added a feather to Red Cloud's hair, and repositioned his braids to hang down the front of his shirt. These not-so-subtle changes suggest the great lengths to which Rinehart went in refiguring portraits to meet the demands of the commercial market.

73. Red Cloud, 1900. Photograph by Frank Rinehart. Private collection.

74. Red Cloud and Pretty Owl with Raymond Smith, 1898. Photograph by Jesse H. Bratley. National Anthropological Archives, Smithsonian Institution, Washington DC (3244).

Red Cloud permitted Bratley to arrange a variety of different views during his visit to Pine Ridge. In one photograph (figure 74), Red Cloud poses beside his wife, Pretty Owl, in front of a tipi and wears an American flag around his shoulders. Behind them stands a mixed-blood named Raymond Smith, wearing a white man's suit and tie. At the time, Smith represented the Oglalas in their interactions with government officials, and in 1898 a group including Smith and Red Cloud had drafted a letter to the commissioner of Indian affairs outlining a list of ongoing grievances. The conclusion of this letter points up the frustration they still harbored:

Our complaints have ever been just, always in the interest of humanity and love, justice and truth. Not until the Sioux Indians are permitted a hearing by the government in the conduct of their own affairs, and mischief-makers that abound so abundantly at all agencies are made to attend strictly to their business, will the Indian problem, which continues to be so agreeably exasperating to the white man, be amenable to wholesome elucidations that will ultimately enable him, in a comparatively short time, to work out his own salvation. We are old enough to be trusted with a voice in the management of our own affairs, and we appeal to all men who are working in the interest of honest government and civilization, and to those high in authority for aid in securing to us that privilege. We are growing weary of looking ahead to that hour of deliverance held in the distance, like a mirage, by oily tongued creatures of greed for power and position, who are above us in political strength, and whose pernicious activity is dooming our hopes of better conditions in this life of disappointment, by bringing down upon our heads the burdens of injustice and misrule under which we have suffered for centuries. We believe that it is the aim of our Commissioner of Indian Affairs, of whom it has been said that he is our friend, to aid us in every possible manner and do away with those things that are harmful to our advancement, and which create in us bitterness of heart and restlessness of mind. The present policy of adding fuel to the flame to keep the pot of discontent boiling will only retard the progress we are expected to make in the march of civilization and occasion unnecessary outbreaks, which is the only way we have of escaping Caesarism and intolerable violations of treaty provisions and promises. . . . . The Sioux Indian at heart is a good man and will make a splendid citizen if only met half way by those who have him in charge, in his inherent desire to do right and be respected. We hope our wishes will be complied with and that our treatment in the future will be on more just, sensible, and humanitarian lines.[11]

Such a letter suggests that Red Cloud wrapped himself in the American flag in an effort to effect positive change for his own people more than to celebrate his allegiance to the United States. Again, he was using photography to commemorate significant collaborations with partners in this effort.

Pine Ridge Agency, South Dakota, 1899

The team of Herman Heyn and James Matzen, with studios in Omaha and Chicago, was another photographic outfit that completed a half-dozen images of Red Cloud as an old man. At the beginning of this session, Red Cloud wears a striped shirt, a leather vest, and a kerchief around his neck (figure 75).

75. Red Cloud, 1899. Photograph by Herman Heyn and James Matzen. National Anthropological Archives, Smithsonian Institution, Washington DC (3238-L).

Later, however, in a seated portrait with Pretty Owl standing beside him, he has put on a finely beaded vest, a breast-plate, and a warbonnet (figure 76). In addition, he now holds his gold-capped cane in one hand and an elaborately carved pipe in the other. Behind the couple, Heyn and Matzen have hung a painted backdrop featuring not the Plains but a woodland scene – again revealing the lengths photographers went to in getting views they wanted, not to mention Red Cloud's willingness to accommodate them.

This series of portraits sold well, and in the following year Heyn and Matzen sold the rights to the Native couple's photograph to the Omaha News Company, which promptly published it as a postcard. The caption on the back gives an idea of how inaccurately non-Natives understood such images: " 'CHIEF RED CLOUD' The last red skin whose authority over his tribe, the Sioux, compelled the U.S. Government to treat with him as the head of a nation. Red Cloud was King over all the Northwest from the Missouri to the Columbia, and during the Black Hills excitement gave frequent evidence of his powers and his magnanimity."[12]

This passage demonstrates not only how Red Cloud's reputation continued to grow within the minds of many Euro-Americans but also how the dominant culture mythologized the history of America's conquest and settlement of the West, dramatically altering both the facts and their significance.

76. Red Cloud with Pretty Owl, 1899. Photograph by Herman Heyn and James Matzen. National Anthropological Archives, Smithsonian Institution, Washington DC (3238-J).

Agate Springs Ranch, Harrison, Nebraska, June 1900

Throughout his life, Red Cloud maintained close relationships with numerous white Americans. One of his best non-Native friends was James H. Cook, a rancher whom he first met in the fall of 1875. Over time, the two men came to trust each other, and several times Red Cloud tried – unsuccessfully – to have Cook appointed agent to the Oglalas. In the aftermath of the tragedy at Wounded Knee he petitioned the commissioner of Indian affairs in March 1891: "You told my people to come home and hold a council and agree on some man whom we all wanted for agent. All my people – men, women, and children – have agreed on one man. That man is James H. Cook of Harrison, Nebraska. He is the choice of us all. We have known him for seventeen years. He is a Western man. He has been among us when we were wild. He knows our nature, our history, and what we want. He is our friend. He will deal justly with us, and help us to learn the ways of the white man. He will treat us as men. We want him and no one else."[13]

Though Indian Bureau officials rejected the request, Red Cloud maintained close ties with Cook. He and Pretty Owl were often guests at Cook's Agate Springs Ranch in Harrison. There, in the spring of 1900, George Gerlach – a Harrison banker and friend of the Cook family – photographed Red Cloud and Pretty Owl (figure 77). Pretty Owl's inclusion in this portrait and others from the period indicates that family increasingly took center stage in Red Cloud's life.

It also reflects an increased interest by non-Natives in his domestic habits. Polygamy had become a topic of national concern during Utah's fight for statehood, which it achieved in 1896, but its campaign for admission had been sidetracked and almost derailed because of the Mormon stance on this issue. Consequently, many within Euro-American society were quick to sensationalize those who maintained personal relationships that fell outside prescribed norms, and articles in the popular press contended that Red Cloud had as many as six wives.[14] Despite these stories, Red Cloud in fact maintained a monogamous household.

Pan-American Exposition, Buffalo, New York, Summer 1901

Accompanied by his longtime friend Charles Jordan, Red Cloud made his last trip east in the summer of 1901 at the age of eighty. Organizers of the 1901 Pan-American Exposition in Buffalo, New York, recruited him to participate in an "Indian Congress and Village," similar to the Indian Encampment in Omaha three years earlier. Though officials hoped that the public would gain "wonderful knowledge . . . from these living pictures," this gathering of seven hundred Native men and women was principally a means of attracting a large audience.[15]

As in Omaha, Native Americans were the centerpiece of numerous displays and demonstrations. Buffalo's rendition, though, in a stadium that held twenty-five thousand people, was even more sensational. Whereas the managers in Omaha had organized only a single sham battle, Buffalo held battles four times a day, including twice at night under electric lights. At the start of the exposition, officials predicted that seven million visi-

78. Red Cloud (*seated, front row, right*) and other members of the "Indian Congress" at the Pan-American Exposition, 1901. Photograph by Charles D. Arnold. Buffalo and Erie County Historical Society, Buffalo NY.

tors would attend the Indian Congress and Village.[16]

Red Cloud did not involve himself in this mock warfare, but he did serve as the lead figure in the daily procession of Native participants into the stadium. In a publicity photograph taken at the entrance of the exhibit (figure 78), the group has turned to face the exposition's official photographer, Charles D. Arnold. Seated in a wheelchair and carrying a guidon, Red Cloud appears to the right at the front of this large group. Reflecting American society's voracious appetite for the "Old West" at the turn of the century, *Pan-American Magazine* commented that "without Native Americans a Pan-American exhibition would be like an old time circus without the clown."[17]

Rosebud Agency, South Dakota, Summer 1902

Though he made no more trips to the East after 1901, Red Cloud continued to remain active. In particular, he spent much time in the nearby town of Chadron, Nebraska, often going there, as he had in the past, to meet friends. Given the attention he received, he seemed to enjoy his excursions outside the reservation.

During the summer of 1902 he took the 110-mile trip with his wife and his grandson to visit Charles Jordan, who was then working as a trader on the adjacent Rosebud reservation. Jordan and Red Cloud had known each other for over twenty years, and the two had often traveled together during that time. According to a newspaper report, Red Cloud wrote the new Pine Ridge agent, Major John R. Brennan, seeking permission to make this journey: "I want to see my good friend of days gone by. . . . I am soon to die and in my last hours I want to once more see the man who has always been my friend." To the reporter covering this event, "it was pathetic to see this broken old man, unkempt and worn, dependent for the necessities of life and led around by the little mite of a four-year-old grandson. The leader of all the allied tribes in a fierce war against the whites because his country was invaded, now shorn of his ancient power and glory even as his long flowing hair was clipped when he buried the tomahawk and took on the habits of the civilized man."[18]

To Red Cloud, though, these excursions seem to have meant a great deal personally. As he had done so often in the past, he marked the occasion by sitting for two portraits, one with Jordan and the other (figure 79) with his grandson.

79. Red Cloud with his grandson, 1902. Photographer unknown. Nebraska State Historical Society, Lincoln (RG2969:1-92).

80. Red Cloud and others, early
1900s. Photograph by John R.
Brennan. Courtesy of South Dakota State Historical Society –
State Archives, Pierre.

Pine Ridge Agency, South Dakota, Early 1900s

In a photograph from an album of views collected by Agent Brennan, Red Cloud stands atop a hay-filled cart and, according to the caption, makes a speech before a gathered audience (figure 80). Most likely, this photograph was taken during a Fourth of July celebration at Pine Ridge. Red Cloud grasps an American flag with one hand while raising his other hand in a dramatic gesture. An unidentified man holds an umbrella over Red Cloud's head to shield him from the sunlight.

Though his decision to hold the American flag in this manner may suggest his acquiescence to the dominant culture, Red Cloud was still a critic of the federal government. Both large tribal issues, such as the future of the Black Hills, and small personal complaints, such as his poor treatment by government officials, could arouse his ire.

This is one of several photographs from these years in which Red Cloud poses holding an American flag or wearing clothes whose design incorporates the Stars and Stripes. For many years the Oglalas protested the American flag as an emblem of oppression. At Red Cloud Agency in October 1874, for example, upset by a series of crises on the reservation, Red Cloud and his supporters entered the courtyard of the new agency and proceeded to chop into pieces the pine pole that government officials had recently selected for use as a flagpole.[19] The flag already flew atop nearby Fort Robinson, and Red Cloud objected to its increased presence on the reservation.

Over the quarter-century since that time, however, the Lakotas had come to appropriate the American flag and its symbolic significance for their own use: instead of an emblem of American patriotism, it became in certain contexts a source of power. Indeed, to possess a flag – or a collection of them, as in Red Cloud's case (see figure 2) – was a sign of one's prowess as a warrior and a statesman. Lakotas who acquired them through war or as gifts understood flags as status symbols that protected those who displayed them.[20]

Though Euro-American officials might see Red Cloud's decision to hold the flag as a symbol of his allegiance to the United States, his fellow Oglalas would have understood its alternative meaning: namely, that Red Cloud was a part of a storied warrior tradition. This moment represents another instance of Red Cloud's ability to wear different faces for different audiences in order to promote good relations. Unlike the resistance of such Lakota leaders as Crazy Horse and Sitting Bull, Red Cloud's activism promoted a possible reconciliation between the two nations.

Also from the Brennan album, figure 81 shows Red Cloud standing among both non-Natives and Oglalas, most of them on horseback. Perhaps an Independence Day parade, common both on and off the reservation, is either about to begin or has just finished.

As opposed to earlier portrait photographs, Red Cloud does not appear to have posed for these two images. Working not in a studio but outdoors with a portable camera, Brennan has successfully captured two instantaneous candid views of the Oglala chief. New photographic technologies, such as George Eastman's Kodak camera, were allowing

81. Red Cloud and others, early 1900s. Photograph by John R. Brennan. Courtesy of South Dakota State Historical Society – State Archives, Pierre.

photographers much greater flexibility.

Brennan's inclusion of these photographs in his personal scrapbook – alongside images of his own family – hint at the respect that the new agent had for Red Cloud. Well aware of the experiences of previous Pine Ridge agents, Brennan seems respectful of the old man.

Pine Ridge Agency, South Dakota, Early 1900s

Though Brennan collected photographs of many Native Americans with whom he worked, no other Oglala's image was as important as Red Cloud's: his three extant photographic albums contained nine different images featuring the old chief. Among them was a portrait (figure 82) made by an unidentified photographer. Holding the same cane as seen in earlier photographs, Red Cloud wears an assortment of beaded objects, including a pair of gauntlets, a tie, and a leather vest. Both the tie and the vest feature a pair of American flags.

By the turn of the century, the flag had attained such significance within Lakota society that it was increasingly incorporated into Native quill and bead work. Again, the appropriation of this distinctly American symbol represented the Lakota effort to subvert the authority of Euro-American society.[21] Prizing flags either captured in battle or given as gifts, a Lakota wore items that included the flag in order to reassert his historic prowess as a great warrior. Not a modest man, Red Cloud carefully nurtured his fame.

Though he appears somewhat at ease in these late photographs, several of his speeches indicate that he remained disillusioned about the fate of his people.

Warren K. Moorehead, an anthropologist and historian who first befriended Red Cloud and his family in the 1890s, transcribed the following statement during this period:

You see this barren waste. . . . Think of it! I, who used to own rich soil in a well-watered country so extensive that I could ride through it in a week on my fastest pony, am put down here! Why, I have to go five miles for wood for my fire. Washington took our lands and promised to feed and support us. Now I, who used to control 5000 warriors, must tell Washington when I am hungry. I must beg for that which I own. If I beg hard, they put me in the guard house. We have trouble. Our girls are getting bad. Coughing sickness every winter carries away our best people. My heart is heavy, I am old, I cannot do much more.[22]

To Red Cloud, these many photographic sessions near the end of his life have dwindled in significance: they serve less as diplomatic exchanges than as perhaps entertaining and, increasingly, moneymaking diversions.

Pine Ridge Agency, South Dakota, September 1903

In September 1903, Red Cloud spoke for the last time in a tribal council meeting. Pine Ridge Agent John R. Brennan was there and photographed the group. South Dakota Congressman Eben W. Martin was also present, ostensibly to hear complaints about the reservation's administration. That non-Natives such as Martin and Brennan were allowed to attend suggests that this meeting was more a public discussion than a traditional closed-door tribal council, but their presence does not

seem to faze the retiring leader in his rocking chair or American Horse, who stands facing the camera (figure 83).

Red Cloud used this opportunity to re-visit the thirty-year-old controversy over the Black Hills, land now thoroughly oc-cupied by American settlers.

Quite a while ago I used some words with the Great Father. It must have been twenty-six or twenty-eight years ago and I have missed most of the words. There was a man came from the Great Father who told me, "Red Cloud, the Great Father told me to come to you because he wants the Black Hills from you." So I asked, "How much money did you bring for the Black Hills?" He answered me, "I brought six million dollars." So I answered him, "This is a little bit of a thing." I told him like this, "The Black Hills is worth to me seven generations, but you give me this word of six million dollars. It is just a little spit out of my mouth." Then he said, "Let me have the Black Hills and the Big Horn both together." But I told him this, "That is too small; so I won't do it." And I kept this land; "So you can go back to the Great Fa-ther and say that to me the Black Hills is worth seven generations. You can tell the Great Father that I will lend him the top of the hills, if he is satisfied, that is what you can tell him. That is just the rocks above the pines." I would like to tell you this my friend; the rations they give us only last for a day. They should give us the money from the Black Hills treaty, because we need it now.[23]

This speech suggests the regret and bitterness he still harbored about his de-cision to sign the Black Hills treaty in 1876. His involvement in that piece of legislation was a black mark on his career as a tribal diplomat, and it continued to trouble him until his death.

83. Red Cloud (*seated, right front*),
American Horse (*standing*), and
others at Red Cloud's last council
meeting, 1903. Photograph by
John R. Brennan. Courtesy of
South Dakota State Historical Society – State Archives, Pierre.

Chief "Red Cloud" and
Freddie Davis
son of-   July 4. 1904
Dr Davis.
                  Chadron
                     Nebr

84. "Chief 'Red Cloud' and
Freddie Davis, Son of Dr. Davis,
July 4, 1904." Photograph by Isiah
R. McIntire. Nebraska State His-
torical Society, Lincoln
(RG2063:19-1).

Studio of Isiah R. McIntire, Chadron, Nebraska, July 4, 1904

Despite his age, Red Cloud continued to pose for local photographers. Among them was Isiah R. McIntire of Chadron, Nebraska, who pictured the chief alongside young Freddie Davis, the son of a local doctor (figure 84). Although Red Cloud places his large hand around the boy's shoulder in a reassuring gesture, the young child, dressed up in a neat white suit and hat, does not seem entirely comfortable.

Red Cloud does not seem to invest this occasion with a larger personal or political significance. For many years he had understood photography as a ritual reserved especially for "official" business. His uncompromisingly stoic expression before the camera reflected that belief. Photographs in which he posed with others could serve as testaments of friendship but were most often the product of some diplomatic exchange. Not until this moment, at the age of eighty-three, did he ever pose with a young child not a member of his family. His willingness to be photographed with Freddie Davis and his friendly embrace of the boy suggest that his approach to photography and his renowned intransigence about other issues were moderating. These late photographs hint at a more conciliatory attitude toward government authorities. For example, after years of refusing to take an allotment as designated under the 1887 Dawes Act, Red Cloud finally agreed in the year this photograph was taken to accept his own plot of land.

Though there may have been other reasons behind his less strident attitude, one factor was certainly his rapidly deteriorating eyesight: by 1904, Red Cloud was almost completely dependent on the assistance of others.

Young Freddie was obviously not alone when he posed for his portrait with Red Cloud. A second photograph shows that many others accompanied them into McIntire's studio. Seated with Red Cloud (figure 85) are Chadron residents Louis Iaeger, Freddie Davis, and Fred Wilke. Standing behind them are Walks Fast, Afraid, Dr. Davis, and George Fire Thunder.

For more than twenty years, non-Natives in Chadron and other nearby towns had invited members of various Lakota communities to participate in festivities related to the Fourth of July holiday. Often these Native groups were paid to present dances and other displays. The Sun Dance had been outlawed for years, but many Oglalas used this occasion to perform a modified version of the holy ritual.

Given his prominence, Red Cloud was always in great demand for such festivities and rarely missed the opportunity to participate. In addition to collecting money and gifts, he often met old acquaintances from outside the reservation. One such individual was Louis Iaeger, a longtime Chadron native who had sat for a portrait with Red Cloud over the Fourth of July holiday fifteen years earlier (figure 46). Hence again they have come together in a local photographer's studio to reaffirm an old friendship. Though Red Cloud might not be able to see everything around him, he must surely have been pleased by this reunion.

85. *Standing, left to right:* Walks Fast, Afraid, Dr. Davis, George Fire Thunder; *seated, left to right:* Louis Iaeger, Freddie Davis, Red Cloud, Fred Wilke, 1904. Photograph by Isiah R. McIntire. Dawes County Historical Society, Chadron NE.

Pine Ridge Agency, South Dakota, 1905

When he met Red Cloud at Pine Ridge in 1905, Edward S. Curtis had recently begun what would become the largest photographic survey of North American Indians ever completed. Supported by President Theodore Roosevelt and underwritten in part by the New York banker J. P. Morgan, Curtis spent almost thirty years traveling to all parts of the North American continent to document Native cultures that he and others believed were vanishing. Curtis generally held Native peoples in high regard and worked to create images that portrayed them in a positive, albeit fading, light.[24]

The elegiac portrait in figure 86 does not rely on fancy studio backdrops or "exotic" Native objects to evoke the idea of Red Cloud's noble bearing. Instead, a single directed ray of light illuminates his head. Though the print's dark background gives the impression that this photograph was taken in low light conditions, a speech Curtis gave two years later at the University of Washington reveals that it was made in "strong sunlight on the open prairie."[25] Whereas Curtis was often concerned about situating his Native subjects in their environmental context, he elected here to pose Red Cloud before a dark backdrop. The decision to remove him from the "open prairie" reflects the photographer's desire to figure Red Cloud as a mythic character from the historical past, rather than as a nameless individual in a setting appropriate to his tribe. With his gray hair and his eyes now closed, Red Cloud represents for Curtis both the glory and the tragedy of Native peoples in America.

It was a great boon for Curtis's project at this early stage that he could hold up Red Cloud as an example from a supposedly unadulterated Native American past. In his introduction to the volume dedicated to the Native people of the Great Plains, first published in 1908, Curtis wrote with a heavy heart his view of the changes he had witnessed while working among these tribes:

Strong sympathy for the Indian cannot blind one to the fact that the change that has come is a necessity created by the expansion of the white population. Nor does the fact that civilization demands the abandonment of aboriginal habits lessen one's sympathy or alter one's realization that for once at least Nature's laws have been the indirect cause of a grievous wrong. That the inevitable transformation of the Indian life has been made many-fold harder by the white man's cupidity, there is no question. . . . The great change that now comes to the Sioux and to other tribes of the plains with the opening of the reservations to settlement and in the consequent increased contact with alien influences will, within the present generation, further demoralize and degenerate. This, however, is one of the stages through which from the beginning the Indians were destined to pass. Those who cannot withstand these trying days of the metamorphosis must succumb, and on the other side of the depressing period will emerge the few sturdy survivors.[26]

Like most Euro-Americans, Curtis saw only cultural extinction in the future for Native Americans.

X1473-05

Pine Ridge Agency, South Dakota, 1905

Taken in the same year as Curtis's photograph, William Crossland's portrait depicts Red Cloud without Curtis's artistry. Less sympathetic but perhaps more honest, this image (figure 87) shows the effects of age and blindness. (Red Cloud wears the same clothes in both portraits; Crossland perhaps accompanied Curtis on his visit to Red Cloud's home.)

As much as the American public was enthralled by stories of Red Cloud's warrior past, so too did they avidly read reports of his imminent death. For some time, newspapers had been writing that Red Cloud was literally on his deathbed. Two years previously, for example, the *Omaha World-Herald* mistakenly announced, "Old, blind, and almost penniless, Red Cloud, chief of the Sioux, lies dying in his little tent at his home. . . . Formerly the greatest of all Indian chieftains, Red Cloud's glory has departed and he lies, a broken reed, dependent on the willing attention of the new generation of red men. White physicians have given up hope of saving the aged sachem's life, and state that dissolution may come at any hour; surely within a few weeks at the most. The medicine men, however, still hold daily pow-wows over their dying chief, and make good medicine in his behalf."[27]

More than simply a sadness about Red Cloud's health, this public fascination with his physical decline perhaps more tellingly revealed the dominant culture's simultaneous attraction and repulsion with regard to an era that, like Red Cloud himself, was slipping away. News from the chief's "deathbed" allowed Euro-Americans to begin the process of closing

87. Red Cloud, 1905. Photograph by William Crossland. National Anthropological Archives, Smithsonian Institution, Washington DC (56398).

once and for all that chapter in the history of the American West. It permitted them both to boast of their supposed achievement and to put behind them any feelings of guilt associated with that "victory."

And yet, though he was not in good health, Red Cloud was not in fact on his deathbed. Time was slowing him down, but he still remained very much alive.

Pine Ridge Agency, South Dakota, 1907

Despite his frail physical condition, Red Cloud continued to sit for the photographer's camera. In a picture taken by Ray W. Graves, he rests on a chair outside a tipi (figure 88), and as on several earlier occasions he wears a feathered headdress, holds a tomahawk in his lap, and grasps an American flag. With him is James R. Walker, the physician at Pine Ridge Agency from 1896 to 1914.

Unlike many previous government doctors assigned to the Oglalas, Walker was unusually successful at building a cooperative relationship with the Native American community. His interest in treating patients in conjunction with tribal medicine men won him widespread support. Cognizant of the devastating effect that tuberculosis was having on Native peoples, he completed extensive studies of its impact on the Oglalas and helped dramatically reduce the number of cases on the reservation.

During his tenure at Pine Ridge, Walker also dedicated himself to learning more about Oglala culture and religion. Encouraged in this pursuit by Clark Wissler, a noted anthropologist associated with the American Museum of Natural History in New York City, Walker con-

88. Red Cloud with James R. Walker, 1907. Photograph by Ray W. Graves. Amon Carter Museum, Fort Worth TX (P1976.1.5.29).

89. Red Cloud and Pretty Owl
(left) with an unidentified man,
1907. Photograph by Ray W.
Graves. Amon Carter Museum,
Fort Worth TX (P1976.1.5.30).

ducted interviews with tribal members, collected examples of the tribe's material culture, and wrote at length about the Oglalas' beliefs and rituals. This research represented the first extensive effort by a Euro-American to study traditional Lakota lifeways. Whereas previous agents and government officials had approached their work with the mandate of "civiliz- ing the Indian," Walker was exceptional in the respect he accorded the Oglalas.[28] As a result, many Oglala elders and holy men, including Red Cloud, trusted the doctor and supported his effort to record and preserve traditional customs.

Though the exact circumstances be- hind this photograph of Walker and Red Cloud are not known, it is consistent with Red Cloud's long tradition of sitting for portraits with those whom he re- spected.

Ray W. Graves had taken over Isiah R. McIntire's commercial photographic stu- dio in Chadron, Nebraska, in November 1906. Like George Trager, Frank Rinehart, and others, Graves sought to make por- traits of notable Native Americans that he hoped to sell to an American public still fascinated by Indian icons such as Red Cloud.

In a second photograph taken by Graves on this occasion, he has moved his camera to document both Red Cloud's two-story house and the tipi (figure 89). With more travelers passing through the area each year, Red Cloud's home was in- creasingly recognized as a significant tourist destination. According to a local newspaper, "A visit to Red Cloud's home, which is about a mile from Pine Ridge Agency and which was built for him about ten years ago by the government, has always been one of the things for offi-

90. *Left to right:* Alexander B. Upshaw, unidentified man, Red Cloud, Edmond S. Meany, Jack Red Cloud, 1907. Photograph by Fred Meyer. MSCUA, University of Washington Libraries, Seattle (NA1478).

cials and visitors to the reservation to do, as a visit here would not be considered complete without seeing this celebrated Oglala Sioux chieftain."[29]

Though Pretty Owl now stands at Red Cloud's side and a third person stands by the fence, the juxtaposition of the two structures seems to be the main intent of this view. In a metaphoric sense it captures the predicament that Red Cloud and other Native Americans faced: situated between a traditional Oglala home and his "white" house, Red Cloud was forever shifting his public identity in an effort to effect positive change for himself and his people.

Pine Ridge Agency, South Dakota, August 1907

When Edward Curtis left Pine Ridge in 1905, he "promised his Indian friends that he would come back and give them a feast in return for which they would reproduce for him an old-time Sioux camp from which should be excluded all the new clothes obtained from the white people."[30]

In August 1907, Curtis and his assistants did return, keenly interested in finishing his book on the Native peoples of the Great Plains. The Seattle photographer brought with him Edmond Meany, a professor of history at the University of Washington, whom he recruited to write a historical sketch of the Lakotas for the volume.[31] Curtis also asked him to obtain a record of Red Cloud's life. According to Meany, "During the interesting interview the feeble old man conferred upon me his own boyhood name of Wah-numpa, or Two Arrows. Coming with this honor to this camp, it was not long until all the Indians were greeting me by the name Wah-numpa."[32]

Also working for Curtis was Alexander B. Upshaw, a member of the Crow tribe who served as an interpreter and a cultural broker. Upshaw had graduated from the Carlisle Indian School in 1897 and came to Curtis's attention through the recommendation of Adolf Muhr, then an assistant to Curtis, who had earlier met Upshaw while working for Frank Rinehart at the 1898 Omaha Exposition. Partially as a result of his Carlisle education, Upshaw believed strongly that assimilation into mainstream culture was the only choice left to Native Americans. When he was not working for Curtis, he taught at the Native American boarding school in Geneo, Nebraska.

Having photographed Red Cloud two years earlier, Curtis himself did not make portraits of the chief on this occasion, choosing to focus instead on more ethnographic scenes. Nevertheless, both Meany (third from left) and Upshaw (far left) are pictured in a group portrait with Red Cloud and his son Jack (far right), taken by amateur photographer Fred Meyer during Curtis's trip to Pine Ridge in August 1907 (figure 90).

91. Red Cloud, 1908. Photograph by Ray W. Graves. Library of Congress, Washington DC.

Studio of Ray W. Graves, Chadron, Nebraska, 1908

Having taken at least five photographs of Red Cloud at Pine Ridge the preceding year, Ray W. Graves obtained more formal portraits of the old chief in his Chadron studio in 1908. In one seated pose (figure 91), Red Cloud wears an elaborately beaded shirt and a feathered headdress. He also proudly displays one of his peace medals.

As this and other photographs suggest, Red Cloud often dressed in all his Native finery during the last years of his life. Though blind at the time, he nonetheless seemed to enjoy the chance to bring out and wear his cherished possessions. It was not simply the items themselves but also the act of putting them on for the photographer that reminded him of his storied past.

Of course, Graves and others were more than happy to accommodate him. Such images were both easy to market and regarded as valuable records of Red Cloud's life. As they had been doing for years, photographers remained intimately involved in the project of gathering materials, images, and information that spoke about Native American history. Euro-Americans, believing that Red Cloud's death would mark the end of an era, were busy doing everything possible to collect items by which to remember him and his people. "For several years everything related to Red Cloud and the history of the Sioux nation in his lifetime has been gathered, including some hundreds of photographs," wrote a local newspaper in 1909. "It is believed the material has been gathered for an adequate account of Red Cloud and his time. And it

is hoped that it may soon be put in form for publication. . . . No Indian chief of the rank of Red Cloud has lived to such an old age as he or witnessed such significant changes upon this continent. Nor has so long maintained his leadership in war and peace."[33]

Euro-Americans were largely blind, however, to the reality of life on the reservation. Important issues involving the tribe's well-being were largely overlooked, as were noteworthy changes that a new generation of Oglala leaders had effected. Photographs such as those taken by Graves say little about the fundamental reorganization of the tribe's economy or the ongoing crisis over political sovereignty. Rather, they confirmed the prevailing stereotypes that the dominant culture harbored.

Questions concerning the future leadership of his tribe still interested Red Cloud at the end of his life. Recognizing his mortality, he remained active during this period in trying to influence the future direction that the tribe would take. One highlight of this effort occurred at Pine Ridge on the Fourth of July 1903 when, with much pomp, Red Cloud formally abdicated his chieftaincy. At this time, James R. Walker, the government doctor assigned to the Oglalas, recorded Red Cloud's speech, which echoes his long-standing frustration with the Americans and his continued allegiance to his tribe:

I was born a Lakota and I have lived a Lakota and I shall die a Lakota. Before the white man came to our country, the Lakotas were a free people. They made their own laws and governed themselves as it seemed good to them. Then they were independent and happy. Then

92. Red Cloud with Jack Red Cloud, 1908. Photograph by Ray W. Graves. Western History Collection, Denver Public Library, Denver CO (X-31566).

they could choose their own friends and fight their enemies. Then men were brave and to be trusted. The white man came and took our lands from us. They put [us] in bonds and made laws for us. We were not asked what laws would suit us. But the white men made the laws to suit themselves and they compel us to obey them. This is not good for an Indian. The white men try to make the Indians white men also. It would be as reasonable and just to try to make the Indians' skin white as to try to make him act and think like a white man. But the white man has taken our territory and destroyed our game so we must eat the white man's food or die. . . . Taku Skanskan (the supernatural patron of moving things) is familiar with my spirit (nagi) and when I die I will go with him. Then I will be with my forefathers. If this is not in the heaven of the white man, I shall be satisfied. The Sun (Wi) is my father. The Wakan Tanka (supernatural power) of the white man has overcome him. But I shall remain true to him. Shadows are long and dark before me. I shall soon lie down to rise no more. While my spirit is with my body the smoke of my breath shall be towards the Sun for he knows all things and knows that I am still true to him.[34]

Having stepped down, Red Cloud proceeded to designate his son Jack as the new head of the Oglalas, but this attempt at conveying authority to his son on the anniversary of American independence was flawed on several levels. For one, leadership among the Lakotas was not traditionally conferred upon an individual by birthright. Even had that practice been legitimate, Red Cloud lacked the political clout to exercise such a transfer of power. Consequently, despite the fact that Jack Red Cloud was held in high regard by his fellow tribesmen, this ceremony ultimately failed.

As in the past, photography provided Red Cloud with the opportunity to assert his importance. In a portrait of father and son posed before a painted studio backdrop (figure 92), Jack rests his hand on his father's shoulder. Photographs such as this suggest that Red Cloud continued to think of himself as at least the ceremonial head of the Oglalas. All the finery and tokens of prestige that he exhibits, though, were not enough to achieve his desired ends.

Agate Springs Ranch, Harrison, Nebraska, May 1908

A frequent visitor to James H. Cook's Agate Springs Ranch, Red Cloud made one last trip there in the spring of 1908 and remained for ten days, visiting and reminiscing with his old friend. Cook was proud of his long association with the fabled chief, proclaiming once that "Red Cloud was my friend for thirty-five years . . . and his friendship for me was, I believe, as genuine as any Indian ever had for a white man."[35] It was Cook who commissioned local photographer Thomas Bean to make a portrait (figure 93) in which Red Cloud poses in his Native finery with five feathers in his hair. A pocket watch and the peace medal given to him by Ulysses S. Grant (see figure 23) hang from his neck.

93. Red Cloud, 1908. Photograph by Thomas Bean. Courtesy, National Museum of the American Indian, Smithsonian Institution, Washington DC.

Red Cloud
Chief of
Sioux Nations.

Bessie Sander Butler
189—

94. "Red Cloud, Chief of the Sioux Nation," 1903. Painting by Bessie Sandes Butler. Agate Fossil Beds National Monument, Harrison NE.

Cook had commissioned others to figure Red Cloud before this time. Five years earlier the Chicago artist Bessie Sandes Butler, a friend of the Cook family, had painted an oil portrait of Red Cloud while the two were at the ranch (figure 94). Picturing Red Cloud as much younger than he was at the time, Butler erased many of the wrinkles in his forehead and gave no indication that he was almost completely blind. These alterations may have been Red Cloud's own suggestions, for he had told another portrait painter during this period to figure him so that "my friends can see me as I looked when I could see."[36] Most likely, the glasses he wears in the Bean photograph were not his but a pair that someone lent him for this portrait. Throughout his life, Red Cloud had definite ideas about how he wanted to be seen.

As a testament to his friendship with Cook, Red Cloud urged him to keep Butler's painting so that future generations might "always go and look at the face of one of the last of the old chiefs that lived before the white men came to take over lands and turn us from the old trails we had followed for so many hundreds of years."[37]

Pine Ridge Agency, South Dakota, July 1909

Though he was blind, somewhat deaf, and partially paralyzed in his last years, Red Cloud continued to attract attention not only from non-Natives in the United States but even from those abroad. In Germany, a nation with a long tradition of studying foreign lands and their indigenous peoples, much interest surrounded Native American culture. This curiosity

during the first decade of the twentieth
century was influenced as much by American popular culture as by the famed careers
of nineteenth-century Prussian scientists
such as Alexander von Humboldt and Karl
Ritter.

Frederick Weygold's 1909 photograph of
Red Cloud (figure 95) represents one manifestation of German interest in Lakota society. Born in a small town outside St. Louis,
Missouri, in 1870 to German immigrant
parents, Weygold was educated at various
schools in Germany before returning to the
United States in 1902. Hoping to become an
artist, he enrolled at the Pennsylvania
Academy of the Fine Arts in Philadelphia,
where he studied for four years. In Philadelphia, an important intellectual center in
the field of ethnology, Weygold spent considerable time pursuing a secondary interest in Plains Indian languages and culture.
In addition, he found that he could supplement his income by helping to place Native
American ethnographic collections in German museums. Initially, he planned to
broker the sales of other people's collections. In 1909, though, he began to acquire
materials himself for resale to museums in
Hamburg and Berlin.[38]

This project explains his appearance on
the Pine Ridge and Rosebud reservations in
July 1909. In addition to collecting Lakota
objects, Weygold brought along a Kodak
box camera to photograph Native individuals and their painted tipis. These photographs accompanied the collection of materials that he ultimately sold to the
Hamburg Museum of Ethnology. He also
kept a set for himself to be used as studies
for his own paintings and illustrated articles.[39]

95. Red Cloud, 1909. Photograph
by Frederick Weygold. Collection
of the Speed Museum of Art, Lou-
isville KY.

As in several other photographs from his last years, Red Cloud – though appearing worn and weary – wears a finely beaded shirt and his much-prized peace medal. His participation in the projects of non-Natives who wanted to preserve aspects of traditional Lakota culture through writing and photographs points to Red Cloud's recurrent desire to reach out to the larger public. To the end of his life he remained a dedicated educator, tribal diplomat, and leader of his people.

Pine Ridge Agency, South Dakota, 1909

Red Cloud posed with his son Jack and Jack's wife, Nancy (figure 96), in the second of two known photographs dated 1909. It is thus one of the last photographic sessions in which Red Cloud participated before his death in the early morning of December 10, 1909. He was buried the next day with the full rites of the Catholic Church in the cemetery at the Holy Rosary Mission. According to Agent Brennan's diary, it snowed heavily that day.

Red Cloud was eighty-eight.

96. Red Cloud with Jack and Nancy Red Cloud, 1909. Photograph by James A. Miller. Courtesy of South Dakota State Historical Society – State Archives, Pierre.

Epilogue

In the fall of 1853, *Harper's New Monthly Magazine* published an "amusing incident" involving a traveling daguerreotype artist, his three assistants, and an unidentified group of Native Americans in the Rocky Mountain West.

They [the travelers] were busily engaged in transferring the strange, wild scene to their metallic plates, when a war-party of Indians suddenly sprang from behind the rocks, and, giving a frightful yell, advanced, with lances poised, ready for battle; when the artist, with a coolness and presence of mind which can not be too much commended, turned towards the advancing party his huge camera, and mystically waving over the instrument, with its apparently death-dealing tube, the black cloths in which his pictures were wrapped, held his lighted cigar in frightful proximity to the dreadful engine, whose "rude throat" threatened to blow away any enemy out of existence!

The savages had heard strange stories of deadly mortars and Paixhan guns, which in one terrific burst could sweep away whole parties of red skins; and panic-stricken, they paused, but for a moment. . . . The strange mortar followed them, its dangerous muzzle ever keeping them in a straight line. Pop! Pop! Pop! went the revolvers from beneath the instrument. . . . The smoke cleared away, and the artists were alone. No time, of course, was lost in rejoining the caravan; and, all danger being over, it became the subject of merriment around the camp-fire, this novel charge upon savage Indians with a daguerreotype instrument.[1]

This narrative represents one of the earliest descriptions of an encounter between Native Americans and photography. Drawing upon Euro-American conceptions of the "Indian" as a superstitious and primitive savage, it helped to establish the notion – which still holds some currency today – that Native Americans were and continue to be fearful of photography. During the next 150 years the popular perception that Native Americans have always cowered before the white man's camera for fear that it would "steal their soul" furthered long-standing racist stereotypes. Although it is true that many Native American communities tried to limit the intrusion of this imaging technology – the Lakotas, for example, have successfully banned any photographs of ceremonial rituals – their resistance has more accurately been part of a larger effort to preserve the autonomy and sanctity of their tribe's cultural and religious life. Many in Euro-American society, however, have figured this hesitancy in terms that serve to maintain the political and social segregation between Native and white America.

Red Cloud's experience suggests that at times, Native peoples – far from being intimidated by the camera – embraced photography as an alternative means of communication. During the latter half of the nineteenth century, a period when America was struggling to solve the "Indian problem" once and for all, a great divide existed between the Lakotas and the United States in regard to their cultural and religious life and their vision of the future. These divergent belief systems, not to mention the language gap, rendered communication difficult even under the most ideal circumstances. In order to settle their differences in a manner other than warfare, they had an urgent need to find additional ways to speak to one another. Although those both behind and before the camera had their separate agendas, photography helped to bridge the divide that separated the two cultures. Few deals were consummated in the photographer's presence, but those sessions allowed for a ceremonial exchange that kept open the lines of communication.

From a cultural perspective, Red Cloud's participation in the ritual of photography suggests how adaptive he and others within Lakota society were to new political circumstances and technological innovations. As anthropologist Raymond J. DeMallie has indicated, the Lakotas do not regard the content and structure of their religious beliefs and rituals as static or monolithic.[2] Instead, traditions are continually changing in order to accommodate new visions and realities. Nontraditional symbols and artifacts have long found a place in the ceremonies and material culture of Native American communities. During the latter half of the nineteenth century, Red Cloud and other leaders recognized the potential significance of photography for them. By incorporating both the photographic ritual and the resulting images into their own culture, they hoped to work out the differences that divided them from Euro-American society.

On a personal level, Red Cloud's embrace of photography supports his often overlooked legacy as a dedicated tribal diplomat during the second half of his life. From the time he emerged on the national scene, Americans had wanted to mythologize Red Cloud as the epitome of Lakota aggressiveness and might. In the days following his death, newspapers across the nation eulogized the fallen chief in exactly these terms. The *Boston Globe*, for example, under the heading "the wiliest enemy of whites in modern times," proclaimed, "From the moment that Red Cloud first emerged from his swaddling clothes until he signed the memorable treaty in 1868, no more skilled warrior or more inveterate enemy of the white race was known in the history of Nebraska. Sitting Bull was more ferocious, Geronimo more cunning in his treachery and more ingenious in his tortures, but Red Cloud exceeded both as a victorious fighter in his battles with the pioneers, the freighters, and the army commands."[3] For his obituary, the *Omaha World-Herald* interviewed an army sergeant who had been stationed at Fort Philip Kearny in August 1867, when Red Cloud and his followers attacked and defeated a group of soldiers they caught outside the safety of the fort. Upon being told that Red Cloud had died, the retired soldier responded, "So Red Cloud is dead, is he? Well, it would have been a blessing had he died forty odd years ago."[4] Rare was the newspaper that even mentioned his long and distinguished career after 1868, as a tribal diplomat dedicated to his tribe's political sovereignty and future welfare.

Those who had spent time with him, though, were more generous in their tributes, often noting his dignity and dedication to a core set of principles. Anthropologist James Mooney, who wrote about the Ghost Dance among the Lakotas and helped to organize the Indian Encampment at the 1898 Trans-Mississippi and International Exposition in Omaha, wrote not long after Red Cloud's death that he had been "a most courtly chief and a natural-born gentleman, with a bow as graceful as that of a Chesterfield."[5] Similarly, Red Cloud's friend James H. Cook portrayed him as a leader worthy of respect: "His right to rule and to oppose the oncoming of the invading paleface, he never doubted. He died as he lived – an Indian who never pretended to be reconstructed. In his prime he was a factor to be dealt with when his country was needed by the white man."[6]

In the years since his death, Red Cloud has remained a figure of great importance among Euro-Americans and Native Americans alike. Though each group has its own set of ideas about his legacy – Lakota communities have long understood him as a much more complicated and controversial figure than have non-Natives – both recognize the power of his reputation to attract attention and respect. To many Americans, Red Cloud's status has remained as mythic after death as it was during his lifetime. In the past century, countless non-Natives have incorporated his name or his image into efforts to achieve their often grandiose ends. During the 1920s, for example, historian Doane Robinson gave birth to the idea of carving Red Cloud's likeness on a face of exposed granite. Hoping to attract tourists to South Dakota, Robinson proposed the creation of a state park in the Black Hills whose centerpiece would be a

monument to the "heroes of the old west" in an area known as the Needles. He envisioned "Custer and his gold-discovering cavalcade winding its way through the Needles, with Red Cloud and a band of Sioux scouts, resentful and suspicious, spying on it through rifts in the pinnacles of the opposite wall, while above, a great mountain buck, wary but unafraid, inspects the pageant with curiosity."[7] Ultimately, this design was scrapped in favor of the faces of Washington, Jefferson, Lincoln, and Roosevelt.

Though Red Cloud's likeness was not included on Mount Rushmore, his photographic portraits have remained very much in circulation, an indication that his image retains its power to convey meaning. As in his own day, however, this meaning has never been fixed but has changed widely according to the different contexts in which the photographs have been situated. In the 1970s, for example, Time-Life Books prominently featured Alexander Gardner's portrait of Red Cloud (figure 9) in their advertisements for a "lusty, rip-roaring new series" of books that told once again "the true story of the old West."[8] For marketing this series to a popular audience, Time-Life editors looked to Red Cloud, pictured with flowing long hair and a scowl on his face, as the quintessential Native American warrior. More recently, the United States Postal Service used Red Cloud's likeness on the ten-cent stamp in a less stereotypical yet still enigmatic manner (figure 97). Issued in August 1987, the Red Cloud stamp was part of a series that aimed to picture more nonwhite faces on the nation's postage. Based loosely on Charles Bell's 1880 photograph (figure 26), the resulting image does nothing to further a

97. Red Cloud stamp. © 1987 United States Postal Service.

fuller understanding of who Red Cloud was. In this diminutive view, the engraver has removed the feather from Red Cloud's hair and made his physiognomy the focus of the stamp. The Indian everyman, Red Cloud has become a blank screen on which viewers can project their own meanings.

To the Lakotas, Red Cloud was neither a stereotype nor a representative example of Native people. Throughout the last century they accorded him a respect that acknowledges both his successes and his failures as warrior and statesman. Given the central role he played for so many years among the Oglalas and his sometimes contradictory statements about a range of issues, his own community's leaders have both lionized and criticized him. Like Euro-American perceptions of him, these feelings reflect as much about contemporary politics as about historical memories. Compared with Crazy Horse and Sitting Bull, two leaders whose lives came to symbolize Lakota resistance following their murders in 1877 and 1890 respectively, Red Cloud and his legacy have been much harder to pin down. His different faces have left many struggling to appreciate him fully. This sentiment is reflected in comments by the anthropologist Warren Moorehead, who worked among the Lakotas at the turn of the century: "One can easily discern that he has done his duty, has defended the claims of the [Lakotas], and been loyal in adversity as in prosperity. It is sad to note that in his declining years his own people are divided against him and seem to lack appreciation of his life and efforts."[9] To some extent, these feelings remain as true today as they were a hundred years ago. Yet his selection for the Nebraska Hall of

Fame and the celebration at the subsequent induction ceremony on May 22, 2001, attest to the sense of pride with which most Lakotas regard him.[10]

Similarly, his photographic portraits continue to be valuable to Native peoples. During the late 1960s, for example, representatives of the American Indian Movement (AIM) completed a popular series of posters featuring important Native American leaders, Red Cloud among them. Interestingly, the photograph that served as the basis of this poster was the same one used by the U.S. Postal Service twenty years later (figure 26). Its popularity is striking, for of the 128 photographs taken of Red Cloud during his lifetime, this is one of the most overtly faux. Wearing a shirt borrowed from the studio's collection and seated in a highly artificial setting, Red Cloud seems to be conspicuously at the mercy of the photographer, Charles Bell. Yet AIM supporters reinvested this same image with a larger political significance. Remembered for his lifelong work in upholding Lakota sovereignty and in resisting Euro-American incursions, Red Cloud became canonized in this poster as a heroic Native American leader. In the context of Native American political culture, the photographer's studio in which Red Cloud sits represents an important battleground on which the historic fight for Native rights and respect has been and continues to be fought. Juxtaposing the two different contexts in which this one image has been situated in the recent past highlights again the ever shifting and highly contested nature of photographic meaning. Despite being products of another century, Red Cloud's portraits continue to be alive with cultural and political significance.[11]

In the context of this book, though, I am most interested in what these photographs suggest about Red Cloud and Lakota-U.S. relations during his lifetime. The late nineteenth and early twentieth centuries can be characterized as a period of great change within both Native American and Euro-American culture. While American authorities solidified their political and economic dominance, Native nations such as the Lakotas fought to control the manner in which change occurred. For a variety of reasons the great majority of Euro-Americans longed to reshape the basic tenets of Native American life to conform with their own popular norms. Missionary and educational initiatives – not to mention political and military campaigns – were dedicated to the cultural replacement of the Native American. The immediate impact on the Lakotas did indeed contribute to widespread political and social changes. It is important to recognize, however, that Native peoples did not sit idly by in the face of these often hostile intrusions. Resistance, as well as accommodation, to such assaults came in many forms. Red Cloud's willingness to participate in the ritual of photography is an important example not of Native peoples' falling into line with what the dominant culture desired but of their appropriating a non-Native technology to respond to new circumstances.

Appendix

Other Photographs of Red Cloud

In the course of my research, I located or learned of 128 different photographs of Chief Red Cloud. It is probable that there are still others, though the number that I missed is likely not great. For this book I selected images that reveal insights into Red Cloud's life. The following photographs are ones I chose not to incorporate. Many are variants of those I have included; some I excluded because I was not able to discover enough information about them or because they were not in good condition. I provide this list, however, for persons interested in tracking them down.

1. Portrait of Red Cloud seated, 1872, by Alexander Gardner. Private collection.

2. Half portrait of Red Cloud, 1877, by Daniel Mitchell. Private collection.

3. Half portrait of Red Cloud, 1880, by Charles Bell. National Museum of the American Indian, Smithsonian Institution, Washington DC (P00477).

4. Half portrait of Red Cloud, 1881 or 1882, by William Cross. Private collection.

5. Portrait of Red Cloud in profile, 1883, by Frank Bowman. Peabody Museum of Natural History, Yale University, New Haven CT.

6. Half portrait of Red Cloud, 1883, by Frank Bowman. Peabody Museum of Natural History, Yale University, New Haven CT.

7. Portrait of Red Cloud, standing, with Othniel Marsh, 1883, by Frank Bowman. Peabody Museum of Natural History, Yale University, New Haven CT.

8. Portrait of Red Cloud, Othniel Marsh, and Ed Laramie, 1883, by Frank Bowman. Peabody Museum of Natural History, Yale University, New Haven CT.

9. Portrait of Red Cloud, Othniel Marsh, Ed Laramie, and Thomas Bostwick, 1883, by Frank Bowman. Peabody Museum of Natural History, Yale University, New Haven CT.

10. Portrait of Red Cloud, his interpreter Mr. Randall, Dr. Thomas A. Bland, and Dr. M. Cora Bland, 1885, by Johnson Brothers. Unlocated (advertised in *Council Fire,* April 1885).

11. Half portrait of Red Cloud with his hat on, by Johnson Brothers, 1885. Unlocated (advertised in *Council Fire,* April 1885).

12. Half portrait of Red Cloud with his hat off, 1885, by Johnson Brothers. Unlocated (advertised in *Council Fire,* April 1885).

13. Portrait of Red Cloud in profile, 1889, by John Nephew. Private collection.

14. Portrait of Red Cloud and Charles Jordan, 1889, by John Nephew. National Anthropological Archives, Smithsonian Institution, Washington DC (3243B-2).

15. Half portrait of Red Cloud, 1889, by John Nephew. National Archives, Washington DC (106-IN-3237-B)

16. Red Cloud and Pretty Owl, 1889, by George Trager and Fred Kuhn. Unlocated (mentioned in Louis Iaeger's diary, Dawes

County Historical Society, Chadron NE).

17. Red Cloud, 1889, by George Trager and Fred Kuhn. Unlocated (mentioned in Louis Iaeger's diary, Dawes County Historical Society, Chadron NE).

18. Portrait of Red Cloud, Major John Burke, and others, 1891, by Clarence Morledge. Western History Collection, Denver Public Library, Denver CO (X-31456).

19. Portrait of Red Cloud, Major John Burke, and others, 1891, by Clarence Morledge. Western History Collection, Denver Public Library, Denver CO (X-31460).

20. Portrait of Red Cloud, American Horse, and Frank North, 1897, by David Barry. Western History Collection, Denver Public Library, Denver CO (B-194).

21. Portrait of Red Cloud, American Horse, and Johnny Baker, 1897, by David Barry. Western History Collection, Denver Public Library, Denver CO (B-196).

22. Portrait of Red Cloud, seated, with American Horse, 1897, by David Barry. Western History Collection, Denver Public Library, Denver CO (B-728).

23. Portrait of Red Cloud, seated, with American Horse, 1897, by David Barry. Western History Collection, Denver Public Library, Denver CO (B-729).

24. Portrait of Red Cloud, American Horse, and others, 1897, by David Barry. Western History Collection, Denver Public Library, Denver CO (B-732).

25. Half portrait of Red Cloud, 1898, by Jesse Bratley. Private collection.

26. Portrait of Red Cloud standing, 1898, by Jesse Bratley. National Museum of the American Indian, Smithsonian Institution, Washington DC (P20993).

27. Portrait of Red Cloud seated, with his pipe, 1898, by Jesse Bratley. National Museum of the American Indian, Smithsonian Institution, Washington DC (P20994).

28. Portrait of Red Cloud, seated, with Pretty Owl, 1898, by Jesse Bratley. Nebraska State Historical Society, Lincoln (1392:27-1).

29. Half Portrait of Red Cloud, 1899, by Herman Heyn and James Matzen. National Anthropological Archives, Smithsonian Institution, Washington DC (3238-I).

30. Portrait of Red Cloud seated, facing right, 1899, by Herman Heyn and James Matzen. National Anthropological Archives, Smithsonian Institution, Washington DC (3238-M).

31. Portrait of Red Cloud seated, facing left, 1899, by Herman Heyn and George Matzen. National Anthropological Archives, Smithsonian Institution, Washington DC (3238-N).

32. Portrait of Red Cloud, seated, with Charles Jordan, 1902, photographer unknown. Unlocated (published in *Omaha World-Herald*, August 31, 1902).

33. Half Portrait of Red Cloud, 1900s, photographer unknown. Unlocated (published in *Omaha World-Herald*, August 9, 1903).

34. Red Cloud and Pretty Owl, early 1900s, by John R. Brennan. South Dakota State Historical Society–State Archives, Pierre.

35. Portrait of Red Cloud and four unidentified men, 1900s, by John R. Brennan. South Dakota State Historical Society–State Archives, Pierre.

36. Portrait of Red Cloud and students from the Geneo Indian School, early 1900s, photographer unknown. National Anthropological Archives, Washington DC (3312-B).

37. Portrait of Red Cloud, M. J. Dolan,

and others at Pine Ridge, early 1900s. Colorado Historical Society, Denver.

38. Portrait of Red Cloud seated on the porch of the Blaine Hotel, early 1900s, by Isiah R. McIntire. Nebraska State Historical Society, Lincoln (R539:24-3).

39. Half Portrait of Red Cloud, c. 1907–9, photographer unknown. Nebraska State Historical Society, Lincoln (A547:1-44).

40. Portrait of Red Cloud, seated, and unidentified white woman, 1907, photographer unknown. Private collection.

41. Portrait of Red Cloud, seated, with unidentified man, 1907, by Ray Graves. Nebraska State Historical Society, Lincoln (1539:24-2).

42. Portrait of Red Cloud, seated, with unidentified man, 1907, by Ray Graves. South Dakota State Historical Society–State Archives, Pierre.

43. Portrait of Red Cloud standing, holding an American flag, 1907, by Ray Graves. South Dakota State Historical Society–State Archives, Pierre.

44. Half portrait of Red Cloud with warbonnet, 1908, by Ray Graves. Nebraska State Historical Society, Lincoln (1392: 11-1).

45. Half portrait of Red Cloud with warbonnet, 1908, by Ray Graves. Western History Collection, Denver Public Library, Denver CO (X-33530).

46. Portrait of Red Cloud, seated, with unidentified man, 1908, by Thomas Bean. Nebraska State Historical Society, Lincoln (1392:39-11).

47. Portrait of Red Cloud, Jack Red Cloud, and others, 1908, by Thomas Bean. Agate Fossil Beds National Monument, Harrison NE.

Notes

Introduction

1. On Sarah Winnemuca's and Chief Joseph's experiences before the camera, see Joanna Cohan Scherer, "The Public Faces of Sarah Winnemuca," *Cultural Anthropology* 3 (May 1988): 178–204; and Mick Gidley, *Kopet: A Documentary Narrative of Chief Joseph's Last Years* (Seattle: University of Washington Press, 1981).

2. In particular, see John Tagg, *The Burden of Representation: Essays on Photographies and Histories* (Minneapolis: University of Minnesota Press, 1993), 34–102.

3. In *Navajo and Photography: A Critical History of the Representation of an American People* (Albuquerque: University of New Mexico Press, 1996), James C. Faris highlights Navajo concern with the practices of non-Native photographers and documents the lengths to which many individuals went in resisting the camera's intrusive eye.

4. Though nineteenth-century tribal communities were generally reluctant to incorporate photography into their rituals and ceremonies, this hesitancy lessened over time. For a good example of Native usage of photography, see Carolyn Marr's "Photographers and Their Subjects on the Southern Northwest Coast: Motivations and Responses," *Arctic Anthropology* 27, no. 2 (1990): 13–26.

5. In *Playing Indian* (New Haven: Yale University Press, 1998), Philip Deloria analyzes Euro-Americans' long-standing interest in bastardizing aspects of Native American culture for their own "playful" use.

6. For an analysis of the collecting impulse, see Susan Stewart, *On Longing: Narratives of the Miniature, the Gigantic, the Souvenir, the Collection* (Durham NC: Duke University Press, 1993).

7. Henry N. Hutchinson, *The Living Races of Mankind* (New York: D. Appleton, 1902), employed 648 photographic illustrations in an attempt to bring all the world's peoples to a popular English and American audience.

8. In particular, see Jane Alison, ed., *Native Nations: Journeys in American Photography* (London: Barbican Art Gallery, 1999); Martha Banta and Curtis Hinsley, *From Site to Sight: Anthropology, Photography, and the Power of Imagery* (Cambridge: Harvard University Press, 1986); Faris, *Navajo and Photography*; Mick Gidley, *Edward S. Curtis and the North American Indian, Incorporated* (New York: Cambridge University Press, 1998); Tim Johnson, ed., *Spirit Capture: Photographs from the National Museum of the American Indian* (Washington DC: Smithsonian Institution Press, 1998); Lucy Lippard, ed., *Partial Recall: Photographs of Native North Americans* (New York: New Press, 1992); and Christopher Lyman, *The Vanishing Race and Other Illusions: Photographs of Indians by Edward S. Curtis* (New York: Pantheon Books, 1982).

9. Pratt has written at length about "contact zones" and "transculturation,"

which is "a term to describe how subordinated or marginal groups select and invent from materials transmitted to them by a dominant or metropolitan culture. While subjugated peoples cannot readily control what emanates from the dominant culture, they do determine to varying extents what they absorb into their own, and what they use it for. Transculturation is a phenomenon of the contact zone." Mary Louise Pratt, *Travel Writing and Transculturation* (New York: Routledge, 1992), 6.

10. Tagg, *Burden of Representation*, 17.

11. For a detailed account of a photographic session in which Red Cloud participated, see "He Faces the Camera: Red Cloud Is Photographed," *New Haven Register* 41 (January 22, 1883): 1.

12. For example, in *On Photography* (New York: Farrar, Straus & Giroux, 1973), 13, Susan Sontag writes, "There is something predatory in the act of taking a picture. To photograph people is to violate them, by seeing them as they never see themselves, by having knowledge of them they can never have; it turns people into objects that can be symbolically possessed. Just as the camera is a sublimation of the gun, to photograph someone is a sublimated murder – a soft murder, appropriate to a sad, frightened time."

13. Roland Barthes, *Camera Lucida: Reflections on Photography* (New York: Hill & Wang, 1981), 27.

14. For more about "mimicry" as a weapon of anticolonial civility, see Homi Bhabha, "Of Mimicry and Man: The Ambivalence of Colonial Discourse," in his volume of essays, *The Location of Culture* (New York: Routledge, 1994), 85–92.

15. In *The Oglala People, 1841–1879: A Political History* (Lincoln: University of Nebraska Press, 1991), historian Catherine Price discusses the manner in which leadership is established and maintained within Oglala culture. She points out that whereas in American society authority "resides in a number of rigidly structured hierarchical offices with fixed terms and clearly defined roles, . . . Oglala concepts of political power and chieftainship were much more fluid" (59–60). Though American officials were always looking to designate a single individual the representative "head chief," the political system of the Oglala opposed the concentration of power in a small group. Instead, many individuals were involved in making decisions for the tribe. Among them, one who could demonstrate authority in a public manner often won the tribe's support.

16. Nell Painter, *Sojourner Truth: A Life, a Symbol* (New York: Norton, 1996), 185–99.

17. For more about late nineteenth-century Lakota drawings, see Janet Berlo, ed., *Plains Indian Drawings, 1865–1935: Pages from a Visual History* (New York: Harry N. Abrams, 1996).

18. William Henry Jackson, *Descriptive Catalogue of Photographs of North American Indians* (Washington DC: Government Printing Office, 1877), 39.

19. Mari Sandoz, *Old Jules* (New York: Hastings House, 1935), 88. Special thanks to Jason Weems for bringing this passage to my attention.

20. Quoted in Leela Gandhi, *Postcolonial Theory: A Critical Introduction* (New York: Columbia University Press, 1998), 149.

21. James Mooney to Doane Robinson, February 28, 1904, in Doane Robinson Papers at the South Dakota State Historical Society – State Archives, Pierre.

22. John Brennan to Doane Robinson,

February 23, 1904, in Robinson Papers.

23. Quoted in Herman J. Viola, *Diplomats in Buckskins: A History of Indian Delegations in Washington City* (Washington DC: Smithsonian Institution Press, 1981), 187.

24. Graham Clarke, Introduction to *The Portrait in Photography*, ed. Graham Clarke (London: Reaktion Books, 1992), 1.

25. For fuller discussion, see Lippard, Introduction to *Partial Recall*, 13–45.

26. Walt Whitman, *November Boughs* (Philadelphia: David McKay, 1888), 74. Whitman began work as a clerk in the Bureau of Indian Affairs in January 1865 but was fired six months later by a newly appointed secretary of the interior who found his *Leaves of Grass* offensive.

27. No autobiography is ever a "true" representation of the self in any absolute sense; one's autobiographical self is always under construction. David H. Brumble, *American Indian Autobiography* (Berkeley: University of California Press, 1988); and Arnold Krupat, *For Those Who Came After: A Study of Native American Autobiography* (Berkeley: University of California Press, 1985), are two important studies of the history and politics of this literary genre as it relates to Native Americans.

28. Concerning ethnologists' use of photography to assist in the codification of racial types during the nineteenth century, see Elizabeth Edwards, "Photographic 'Types': The Pursuit of Method," *Visual Anthropology* 3, nos. 2–3 (1990): 235–58. For analysis of the range of stereotypes that Euro-Americans have assigned to photographs of Native Americans, see Rick Hill, "High-Speed Film Captures the Vanishing American, in Living Color," *American Indian Culture and Research Journal* 20, no. 3 (1996): 111–28.

29. Red Cloud has been the subject of three biographies, each of which uses conventional Euro-American methodologies to recount his life. The earliest is George E. Hyde, *Red Cloud's Folk: A History of the Oglala Sioux Indians* (Norman: University of Oklahoma Press, 1937), which focuses primarily on the first half of his life. James C. Olson, *Red Cloud and the Sioux Problem* (Lincoln: University of Nebraska Press, 1965), though it considers his life more fully, concentrates most notably on his political and military relationship with the U.S. government. The most recent biography is Robert W. Larson, *Red Cloud: Warrior-Statesman of the Lakota Sioux* (Norman: University of Oklahoma, 1997). Having incorporated a number of recently discovered sources, including most significantly a series of autobiographical statements, Larson has written the most complete biography to date.

30. Price, *The Oglala People*, ix.

31. In his old age, Red Cloud told an interviewer that he had seen action in eighty battles. R. Eli Paul, introduction to *Autobiography of Red Cloud: War Leader of the Oglalas*, ed. R. Eli Paul (Helena: Montana Historical Society Press, 1997), 11.

32. "The Fate of a Frank Leslie 'Special,'" *Frank Leslie's Illustrated Newspaper* 23 (October 27, 1866): 94.

33. Price, *The Oglala People*, 59.

34. These events are chronicled in greater detail in Olson, *Red Cloud*, and Larson, *Red Cloud*.

35. "Meeting of the Indian Commission, at Cooper Institute, New York City," *Frank Leslie's Illustrated Newspaper* 30 (July 2, 1870): 247.

36. "Sioux Chiefs and Warriors," *Frank Leslie's Illustrated Newspaper* 30 (July 9, 1870): 261.

37. Paul, introduction to *Autobiography of Red Cloud*, 10–11.

38. Previous historians have suggested that Red Cloud felt he had never been given the respect he deserved. See Royal B. Hassrick, *The Sioux: Life and Customs of a Warrior Society* (Norman: University of Oklahoma Press, 1964), 14.

1. First Exposure, 1870–1877

1. "The Indians at the White House," *Washington Evening Star* 39 (May 28, 1872): 1.

2. Quoted in James W. Daniels to Francis A. Walker, April 11, 1872, Bureau of Indian Affairs Collection, National Anthropological Archives, Smithsonian Institution, Washington DC.

3. See Mark D. Katz, *Witness to an Era: The Life and Photographs of Alexander Gardner* (New York: Viking Penguin, 1991).

4. See Colin Taylor, *"Ho, for the Great West": The West of William Blackmore* (London: Eatome, 1980). On Blackmore's support of a photographic archive of Native Americans, see Paula Fleming and Judith Luskey, *Grand Endeavors of American Indian Photography* (Washington DC: Smithsonian Institution Press, 1993), 21–23.

5. "Sioux Chiefs and Warriors," 261.

6. Warren K. Moorehead, *The American Indian in the United States* (Andover MA: Andover Press, 1914), 179.

7. Quoted in Herbert Oliver Brayer, ed., "Exploring the Yellowstone with Hayden, 1872: The Diary of Sidford Hamp," *Annals of Wyoming* 14 (October 1942): 262.

8. Jackson, *Descriptive Catalogue*, 39.

9. "The Sioux Chiefs," *Omaha Republican* 17 (May 13, 1875): 4.

10. Walter G. Marshall, a British travel writer who journeyed by rail from New York City to San Francisco during the summer of 1878, met Julius Meyer and spent two days with him in Omaha. His published journal speaks at some length about Meyer: *Through America; or, Nine Months in the United States* (London: S. Low, Marston, Searle & Rivington, 1881), 113–18.

11. Julius Sterling Morton, *Illustrated History of Nebraska*, 3 vols. (Lincoln: J. North, 1906), 2:234. My thanks to John Carter for bringing this citation to my attention.

12. Quoted in *Report of the Commission Appointed to Treat with the Sioux Indians for the Relinquishment of the Black Hills* (Washington DC: Government Printing Office, 1875), 8.

13. "The Last Indian Council," *Washington Evening Star* 45 (June 5, 1875): 1.

14. "Dakota News," *Yankton Daily Press and Dakotaian* 2 (December 15, 1876): 4.

15. Julie Brown, *Contesting Images: Photography and the World's Columbian Exposition* (Tucson: University of Arizona Press, 1994), 10.

16. Another indication of his popularity at this time is the fact that at least two ship companies named vessels after him. In November 1877, owners of a newly built merchant ship in Boston named it the *Red Cloud* and mounted as a figurehead a carved image of the chief. Even in the West, where Native Americans continued to be perceived as a threat, a steamboat company along the Missouri River also thought enough of Red Cloud to name a new riverboat after him. Frederick C. Matthews, *American Merchant Ships, 1850–1900*, Ser. 2 (Salem MA: Marine Research Society, 1931), 270–71.

17. Quoted in Albert G. Brackett, "The Sioux or Dakota Indians," in *Annual Report of the Board of Regents of the Smithsonian In-*

stitution (Washington DC: Government Printing Office, 1877), 466.

18. *Wyoming Weekly Leader* 10 (September 13, 1877): 2.

19. "Sioux Warriors in New York City," *Frank Leslie's Illustrated Newspaper* 45 (October 20, 1877): 107.

2. The Path of Diplomacy, 1877–1880

1. "Wyoming Is Free," *Wyoming Weekly Leader* 11 (October 18, 1877): 2.

2. "Red Cloud in an Ugly Temper," *New York Times* 27 (July 15, 1878): 1.

3. See Arval Looking Horse, "The Sacred Pipe in Modern Life," in *Sioux Indian Religion: Tradition and Innovation*, edited by Raymond J. DeMallie and Douglas R. Parks (Norman: University of Oklahoma Press, 1987); and James Walker, *Lakota Belief and Ritual*, edited by Raymond J. DeMallie and Elaine A. Jahner (Lincoln: University of Nebraska Press, 1980), for analysis of the pipe's importance in Lakota culture.

4. See Francis Paul Prucha, *Indian Peace Medals in American History* (Madison: State Historical Society of Wisconsin, 1971).

5. "Speech of Red Cloud, Chief of the Oglalla Sioux, Two Years Ago," *Council Fire* 3 (March 1880): 37.

6. "Straight Talk by a Straight Tongued Sioux Chief," *Council Fire* 2 (February 1879): 27.

7. Julia B. McGillycuddy, *McGillycuddy, Agent* (London: Oxford University Press, 1941), 6, 188.

8. "Indians as Temperance Talkers," *Washington Post*, no. 796 (June 14, 1880): 1. Ever critical of Red Cloud, Agent McGillycuddy hinted on occasion that the Oglala chief did not always live up to his pronoucements on this subject. In his 1881 annual report to the commissioner of Indian affairs, he wrote that "this taste and desire for liquor appears not alone among the common Indians; it is not unwelcome to even Red Cloud, . . . for excessive use of the fluid which exhilerates [*sic*] and at the same time intoxicates has had much to do with eliminating what grandeur formerly existed in this Indian, and has resulted in his downfall among his people." Quoted in *Report of the Commissioner of Indian Affairs* (Washington DC: Government Printing Office, 1881), 45.

9. "Not in War Costume," *New Haven Evening Register* 41 (January 20, 1883): 1.

10. "The Studios of America," *Photographic Times and American Photographer* 13 (September 1883): 474.

11. For more about photography's incorporation in the field of anthropology, see Curtis Hinsley and Martha Banta, *From Site to Sight: Anthropology, Photography, and the Power of Imagery* (Cambridge: Harvard University Press, 1986); and Elizabeth Edwards, ed., *Anthropology and Photography, 1860–1920* (New Haven: Yale University Press, 1994).

12. Quoted in Gay Waters, *The Poetical Works of Gay Waters, Including the Wicota* (Cincinnati: Standard, 1887), 143–44.

13. During this period the anthropology community was fascinated by photography's potential to assist research into the study of human development and racial composition. In addition to the myriad portraits taken of Native American men, women, and children, at least one anthropologist experimented with composite portraits, seeking to determine the average size of a particular tribe's skull by combining photographic negatives of multiple members of the same tribe. See Alice C. Fletcher, "Composite

Portraits of American Indians," *Science* 7 (May 7, 1886): 408. On photography as a measuring device, see Frank Spencer, "Some Notes on the Attempt to Apply Photography to Anthropometry during the Second Half of the Nineteenth Century," in Edwards, *Anthropology and Photography*, 99–107.

14. Quoted in Jackson, *Descriptive Catalogue*, iii–iv.

3. Playing the American, 1881–1889

1. Quoted in *Annual Report of the Commissioner of Indian Affairs, 1880* (Washington DC: Government Printing Office, 1882), 162.

2. "Surrender of Sitting Bull," *Washington Evening Star* 58 (July 2, 1881): 2.

3. "The Indian Love-Feast," *Washington Post*, no. 1227 (August 20, 1881): 1.

4. "Red Cloud and His Horses," *Council Fire* 6 (January 1883): 3–4.

5. Richard Pratt to Hiram Price, October 13, 1880, Bureau of Indian Affairs Collection, Washington DC.

6. John C. Ewers, *Teton Dakota Ethnology and History* (Berkeley: United States National Park Service, 1938), 23.

7. "Chief Red Cloud Makes Last Visit to His Friend, Col. Charles P. Jordan," *Omaha World-Herald* 37 (August 31, 1902): 22.

8. Paul Steinmetz, *Pipe, Bible, and Peyote among the Oglala Lakota: A Study in Religious Identity* (Knoxville: University of Tennessee Press, 1990), 35.

9. For a study of photography's place at Richard H. Pratt's Carlisle Indian School, see Lonna Malmsheimer, " 'Imitation White Man': Images of Transformation at the Carlisle Indian School," *Studies in Visual Communication* 11 (fall 1985): 54–75.

10. "Red Cloud," *Carlisle Herald*, February 8, 1883, 2.

11. "A Visit from Red Cloud," *Southern Workman* 12 (February 1883): 19.

12. *Report of the Commissioner of Indian Affairs* (Washington DC: Government Printing Office, 1885), 34.

13. Red Cloud refused to allow Marsh's party to reach its destination in the Badlands until the Yale scientist promised to submit his complaints in person to the president of the United States. See Othniel C. Marsh, "A Statement of Affairs at Red Cloud Agency, Made to the President of the United States," pamphlet dated 1875 in the Anthropology Library of the National Museum of Natural History, Washington DC.

14. "Red Cloud Visits a Friend," *New York Times* 32 (January 21, 1883): 1.

15. "An Indian Guest," *Yale Daily News* 6 (January 22, 1883): 1, 4.

16. "He Faces the Camera," 1.

17. "He Faces the Camera," 1.

18. Frank A. Bowman to Othniel Marsh, June 15, 1883, receipt in Othniel Marsh Papers, Manuscript and Archives, Yale University Library, New Haven CT.

19. "Chief Mapah Alutah (Red Cloud)," *Council Fire and Arbitrator* 7 (October 1884): 140.

20. "Washington News and Gossip," *Washington Evening Star* 61 (February 24, 1883): 1.

21. "Our Reception to Chief Red Cloud," *Council Fire and Arbitrator* 8 (April 1885): 54.

22. "President and Cabinet," *Washington Post*, no. 2532 (March 19, 1885): 1.

23. "Honoring Red Cloud," *Council Fire and Arbitrator* 8 (April 1885): 58.

24. "Chief Red Cloud Makes a 4th of July Speech," *Council Fire* 9 (August–September 1886): 125.

25. Quoted in Patricia N. Limerick, *The Legacy of Conquest: The Unbroken Past of the American West* (New York: Norton, 1987), 198.

26. Ewers, *Teton Dakota Ethnology*, 25.

4. Wounded Knee and Its Aftermath, 1889–1897

1. Lynn Marie Mitchell, "George E. Trager: Frontier Photographer at Wounded Knee," *History of Photography* 13 (October–December 1989): 303.

2. "The Celebration," *Chadron Democrat* 4 (July 4, 1889): 1.

3. Louis John Frederick Iaeger, *Man of Many Frontiers: The Diaries of "Billy the Bear" Iaeger* (Omaha: Making History, 1994), 448.

4. Quoted in James P. Boyd, *Recent Indian Wars* (Philadelphia: Publishers Union, 1891), 181.

5. Many thanks to Don Tenoso for pointing out this fact.

6. Jonathan Baxter Harrison, *The Latest Studies on Indian Reservations* (Philadelphia: Indian Rights Association, 1887), 17.

7. Charles Eastman, *From the Deep Woods to Civilization* (Lincoln: University of Nebraska Press, 1977), 100.

8. Quoted in Richard E. Jenson, R. Eli Paul, and John Carter, *Eyewitness at Wounded Knee* (Lincoln: University of Nebraska Press, 1991), 73.

9. Quoted in Thomas A. Bland, ed., *A Brief History of the Late Military Invasion of the Home of the Sioux* (Washington DC: National Indian Defense Association, 1891), 20.

10. George Bird Grinnell, "The Massacre of Big Foot's Band," *New York Tribune* 50 (January 4, 1891): 2.

11. Jenson, Paul, and Carter, *Eyewitness*, 40. One observer wrote that "photogra-phers are 'thicker' about this place than you can imagine and are doing a big business." John V. Lauderdale to Josephine L. Lauderdale, January 11, 1891, John V. Lauderdale Papers, Yale Collection of Western Americana, Beinecke Rare Book and Manuscript Library, New Haven CT.

12. William Coleman, *Voices of Wounded Knee* (Lincoln: University of Nebraska Press, 2000), 339, 368–69.

13. Quoted in "In the Bad Lands," *Harper's Weekly* 35 (January 10, 1891): 18–19.

14. George Bartlett to Othniel Marsh, February 24, 1891, Marsh Papers.

15. Eastman, *From the Deep Woods*, 95.

16. Red Cloud, George Fire Thunder, and Raymond Smith to William A. Jones, June 24, 1898, Indian Rights Association Papers, Historical Society of Pennsylvania, Philadelphia.

17. *Statements of Oglalla Sioux before the Chairman of the Committee on Indian Affairs, United States Senate*, 55th Cong., 1st sess., 1897, S. Doc. 61, 10.

18. "President Meets American Horse," *Washington Post*, no. 6631 (May 4, 1897): 7.

19. Elbridge Burbank to Edward E. Ayer, July 9, 1899, Edward E. Ayer Archive, Newberry Library, Chicago. My thanks to Melissa Wolfe for pointing me to this collection.

20. See Thomas Heski, *"Icastinyanka Cikala Hanzi": The Little Shadow Catcher: D. F. Barry, Celebrated Photographer of Famous Indians* (Seattle: Superior, 1978).

21. For a detailed analysis of the importance of the "Old West" in turn-of-the-century American visual culture, see Alex Nemerov, "Doing the 'Old America': The Image of the American West, 1880–1920," in *The West as America: Reinterpreting Images of the Frontier, 1820–1920*, edited by

William H. Truettner (Washington DC: Smithsonian Institution Press, 1991), 285–343.

22. Quoted in Richard Slotkin, "The 'Wild West,'" in *Buffalo Bill and the Wild West* (exhibition catalogue, Brooklyn Museum, 1981), 34.

5. The Icon, 1898–1909

1. James B. Haynes, *History of the Trans-Mississippi and International Exposition of 1898* (St. Louis: Woodward & Tiernan, 1910), 221.

2. James Mooney, "The Indian Congress at Omaha," *American Anthropologist* 1 (January 1899): 128.

3. "New Red Men and Native Tribes at Exposition," *Omaha World-Herald* 33 (August 11, 1898): 4.

4. "Red Men Avoid the Battle," *Omaha World-Herald* 33 (August 11, 1898): 5.

5. Haynes, *History of the Trans-Mississippi*, 231–32.

6. My thanks to Peter Nabokov for pointing out this fact.

7. Mooney, "Indian Congress," 147.

8. Ira Jacknis, "James Mooney as an Ethnographic Photographer," *Visual Anthropology* 3, nos. 2–3 (1990): 183.

9. Red Cloud to William A. Jones, April 27, 1898, Indian Rights Association Papers.

10. Veronica Dolen, "Life on the Reservation," *Denver Post Empire Magazine* 86 (November 6, 1977): 17–23.

11. Red Cloud, George Fire Thunder, and Raymond Smith to William A. Jones, June 24, 1898, Indian Rights Association Papers.

12. Postcard in the Photographic Collection of the Nebraska State Historical Society, Lincoln.

13. Quoted in James H. Cook, *Fifty Years on the Old Frontier* (Norman: University of Oklahoma Press, 1980), 173.

14. Olson, *Red Cloud*, 23.

15. Frederick T. Cummins, *Historical Biography and Libretto of the Indian Congress*, pamphlet in the Anthropology Library of the National Museum of Natural History, Washington DC.

16. Cummins, *Historical Biography*, n.p.

17. Quoted in Thomas E. Leary and Elizabeth C. Sholes, *Buffalo's Pan-American Exposition* (Charleston SC: Arcadia, 1998), 107.

18. "Chief Red Cloud Makes Last Visit to His Friend, Col. Charles P. Jordan," *Omaha World Herald* 37 (August 31, 1902): 22.

19. Charles Allen provides an eyewitness account of this incident in "Red Cloud and the U.S. Flag," *Nebraska History* 22 (January–March 1941): 77–88.

20. Two books, in particular, have explored the iconography of the American flag in Native American society and material culture: Richard A. Pohrt, *The American Indian and the American Flag* (Flint MI: Flint Institute of the Arts, 1975); and Toby Herbst and Joel Kopp, *The Flag in American Indian Art* (Seattle: University of Washington Press, 1993).

21. Howard Bad Hand, "The American Flag in Lakota Tradition," in Herbst and Kopp, *The Flag in American Indian Art*, 11–13.

22. Moorehead, *American Indian*, 186.

23. Quoted in Olson, *Red Cloud*, 337–38.

24. Edward Curtis's photographic work has been the subject of much scholarly debate in the recent past. The most definitive analysis to date is Gidley, *Edward S. Curtis*. See also Lyman, *The Vanishing Race*; and Bill Holm and George Irving Quimby, *Edward S. Curtis in the*

Land of the War Canoes: A Pioneer Cinematographer in the Pacific Northwest (Seattle: University of Washington Press, 1980).

25. Quoted in Gidley, *Edward S. Curtis*, 79.

26. Edward S. Curtis, introduction to *The North American Indian*, 20 vols. (Cambridge: University Press, 1908), 3:xii–xiii.

27. T. R. Porter, "Famous Sioux Chief, Red Cloud, Lies on His Death Bed at Pine Ridge Agency," *Omaha World-Herald* 39 (August 9, 1903): 19.

28. Walker, *Lakota Belief*, 3–61.

29. "Red Cloud: A Brief History," *Oglala Light* 10 (December 1909): 246.

30. Edmond S. Meany, "Curtis Obtains Rare Plates," *Seattle Times*, August 11, 1907, 25.

31. Gidley, *Edward S. Curtis*, 181.

32. Meany, "Curtis Obtains Rare Plates," 25.

33. "Chief Red Cloud Dead," *Chadron Journal* 26 (December 17, 1909): 9.

34. Quoted in Walker, *Lakota Belief*, 138, 140.

35. Cook, *Fifty Years*, 207, 186.

36. Quoted in Ernest Royce, *Burbank among the Indians* (Caldwell ID: Caxton Printers, 1944), 128.

37. Red Cloud to James H. Cook, May 13, 1908, James H. Cook Papers at Agate Fossil Beds National Monument, Harrison NE.

38. Wolfgang Haberland, *Ich, Dakota* (Berlin: Reimer, 1986), 43–44.

39. Haberland, *Ich, Dakota*, 44–46.

Epilogue

1. "Editor's Drawer," *Harper's New Monthly Magazine* 7 (November 1853): 851.

2. Raymond J. DeMallie, "Lakota Belief and Ritual in the Nineteenth Century," in DeMallie and Parks, *Sioux Indian Religion*, 43.

3. "Red Cloud Gone to Final Rest," *Boston Globe* 76 (December 11, 1909): 2.

4. "Famous Chief Red Cloud Dead at Pine Ridge Agency," *Omaha World-Herald* 45 (December 11, 1909): 1.

5. James Mooney, "Red Cloud," in *The Handbook of American Indians North of Mexico*, edited by Frederick W. Hodge (Washington DC: Government Printing Office, 1910), 359.

6. Cook, *Fifty Years*, 209.

7. Quoted in Rex Alan Smith, *The Carving of Mount Rushmore* (New York: Abbeville Press, 1985), 26–27.

8. Advertisement for Time-Life Books, *Popular Science Monthly* 203 (November 1973): 12.

9. Warren Moorehead, "Life of Red Cloud," manuscript in the Eli Ricker Collection, Nebraska State Historical Society, Lincoln.

10. My thanks to Charles Trimble for information about this designation.

11. Despite the great popularity of photographs of nineteenth-century Native Americans, little has been written on the use and reappropriation of these images in the twentieth century – a field ripe for future scholarship.

Selected Bibliography

Adams, David. *Education for Extinction: American Indians and the Boarding School Experience, 1875–1928*. Lawrence: University Press of Kansas, 1995.

Alison, Jane, ed. *Native Nations: Journeys in American Photography*. London: Barbican Art Gallery, 1999.

Aperture Foundation, Inc. *Strong Hearts: Native American Visions and Voices. Aperture*, no. 139 (1995).

Banta, Martha, and Curtis Hinsley. *From Site to Sight: Anthropology, Photography, and the Power of Imagery*. Cambridge: Harvard University Press, 1986.

Barthes, Roland. *Camera Lucida: Reflections on Photography*. New York: Hill & Wang, 1981.

Bhabha, Homi. *The Location of Culture*. New York: Routledge, 1994.

Blackman, Margaret B. " 'Copying People': Northwest Coast Native Response to Early Photography." *B.C. Studies*, no. 52 (winter 1981–82): 86–112.

Blackstone, Sarah. *Buckskins, Bullets, and Business: A History of Buffalo Bill's Wild West*. New York: Greenwood Press, 1986.

Brown, Julie. *Contesting Images: Photography and the World's Columbian Exposition*. Tucson: University of Arizona Press, 1994.

Brumble, H. David. *American Indian Autobiography*. Berkeley: University of California Press, 1988.

Bush, Alfred, and Lee Mitchell. *The Photograph and the American Indian*. Princeton: Princeton University Press, 1994.

Clarke, Graham, ed. *The Portrait in Photography*. London: Reaktion Books, 1992.

Coleman, William. *Voices of Wounded Knee*. Lincoln: University of Nebraska Press, 2000.

Deleuze, Gilles, and Felix Guattari. *A Thousand Plateaus: Capitalism and Schizophrenia*. Minneapolis: University of Minnesota Press, 1987.

Deloria, Philip. *Playing Indian*. New Haven: Yale University Press, 1998.

DeMallie, Raymond J., and Douglas R. Parks, eds. *Sioux Indian Religion: Tradition and Innovation*. Norman: University of Oklahoma Press, 1987.

Dippie, Brian. *The Vanishing American: White Attitudes and U.S. Indian Policy*. Lawrence: University Press of Kansas, 1982.

Edwards, Elizabeth, ed. *Anthropology and Photography, 1860–1920*. New Haven: Yale University Press, 1994.

Ewers, John C. *Teton Dakota Ethnology and History*. Berkeley: U.S. National Park Service, 1938.

Faris, James. *Navajo and Photography: A Critical History of the Representation of an American People*. Albuquerque: University of New Mexico Press, 1996.

Fleming, Paula, and Judith Luskey. *Grand Endeavors of American Indian Photography*. Washington DC: Smithsonian Institution Press, 1993.

———. *The North American Indians in Early Photographs*. New York: Harper & Row, 1986.

Gandhi, Leela. *Postcolonial Theory: A Critical Introduction.* New York: Columbia University Press, 1998.

Gidley, Mick. *Edward S. Curtis and the North American Indian, Incorporated.* New York: Cambridge University Press, 1998.

———. *Kopet: A Documentary Narrative of Chief Joseph's Last Years.* Seattle: University of Washington Press, 1981.

Goetzmann, William. *The First Americans: Photographs from the Library of Congress.* Washington DC: Starwood, 1991.

Greenblatt, Stephen. *Marvelous Possessions: The Wonder of the New World.* Chicago: University of Chicago Press, 1991.

Gross, Larry, John S. Katz, and Jay Ruby, eds. *Image Ethics: The Moral Rights of Subjects in Photographs, Film, and Television.* New York: Oxford University Press, 1988.

Hassrick, Royal. *The Sioux: Life and Customs of a Warrior Society.* Norman: University of Oklahoma Press, 1964.

Hyde, George. *Red Cloud's Folk: A History of the Oglala Sioux Indians.* Norman: University of Oklahoma Press, 1937.

Jacknis, Ira, ed. *American Indian Culture and Research Journal.* Los Angeles: American Indian Studies Center, 1996.

Jensen, Richard E., R. Eli Paul, and John E. Carter. *Eyewitness at Wounded Knee.* Lincoln: University of Nebraska Press, 1991.

Johnson, Tim, ed. *Spirit Capture: Photographs from the National Museum of the American Indian.* Washington DC: Smithsonian Institution Press, 1998.

Johnston, Patricia, ed. *Exposure Special Issue: "Native American Photography."* Dallas TX: Society for Photographic Education, 1993.

Krupat, Arnold. *For Those Who Come After: A Study of Native American Autobiography.* Berkeley: University of California Press, 1985.

———, ed. *Native American Autobiography: An Anthology.* Madison: University of Wisconsin Press, 1994.

Larson, Robert W. *Red Cloud: Warrior-Statesman of the Lakota Sioux.* Norman: University of Oklahoma Press, 1997.

Lesy, Michael. *Bearing Witness: A Photographic Chronicle of American Life, 1860–1945.* New York: Pantheon Books, 1982.

Limerick, Patricia. *The Legacy of Conquest: The Unbroken Past of the American West.* New York: Norton, 1987.

Lippard, Lucy, ed. *Partial Recall: Photographs of Native North Americans.* New York: New Press, 1992.

Lyman, Christopher. *The Vanishing Race and Other Illusions: Photographs of Indians by Edward S. Curtis.* New York: Pantheon Books, 1982.

Masayesva, Victor, and Erin Younger. *Hopi Photographers, Hopi Images.* Tucson: University of Arizona Press, 1983.

Mellon, James. *The Face of Lincoln.* New York: Viking Press, 1979.

Moses, Lester G. *Wild West Shows and the Images of American Indians, 1883–1933.* Albuquerque: University of New Mexico Press, 1996.

Olson, James. *Red Cloud and the Sioux Problem.* Lincoln: University of Nebraska Press, 1965.

Painter, Nell. *Sojourner Truth: A Life, a Symbol.* New York: Norton, 1996.

Panzer, Mary. *Mathew Brady and the Image of History.* Washington DC: Smithsonian Institution Press, 1997.

Paul, R. Eli, ed. *The Autobiography of Red Cloud: War Leader of the Oglalas.* Helena: Montana Historical Society Press, 1997.

Powers, William. *Oglala Religion*. Lincoln: University of Nebraska Press, 1975.

Pratt, Mary Louise. *Travel Writing and Transculturation*. New York: Routledge, 1992.

Price, Catherine. *The Oglala People, 1841–1879: A Political History*. Lincoln: University of Nebraska Press, 1996.

Prucha, Francis. *American Indian Policy in Crisis: Christian Reformers and the Indian, 1865-1900*. Norman: University of Oklahoma Press, 1976.

Reddin, Paul. *Wild West Shows*. Urbana: University of Illinois Press, 1999.

Rugg, Linda H. *Picturing Ourselves: Photography and Autobiography*. Chicago: University of Chicago Press, 1997.

Ryan, James R. *Picturing Empire: Photography and the Visualization of the British Empire*. Chicago: University of Chicago Press, 1997.

Sandweiss, Martha, ed. *Photography in Nineteenth-Century America*. New York: Harry N. Abrams, 1991.

Scherer, Joanna Cohan. "The Public Faces of Sarah Winnemucca." *Cultural Anthropology* 3, no. 2 (1988): 178–204.

———. "You Can't Believe Your Eyes: Inaccuracies in Photographs of North American Indians." *Exposure* 16 (winter 1978): 6–19.

———, ed. *Visual Anthropology* Special Issue: "Public Cultures: Historic Photographs in Anthropological Inquiry." New York: Harwood Academic Publishers, 1990.

Sekula, Allan. *Photography against the Grain*. Halifax: Nova Scotia College of Art and Design, 1984.

Smith, Shawn. *American Archives: Gender, Race, and Class in Visual Culture*. Princeton: Princeton University Press, 1999.

Sontag, Susan. *On Photography*. New York: Farrar, Straus & Giroux, 1973.

Steinmetz, Paul. *Pipe, Bible, and Peyote among the Oglala Lakota: A Study in Religious Identity*. Knoxville: University of Tennessee Press, 1990.

Stewart, Susan. *On Longing: Narratives of the Miniature, the Gigantic, the Souvenir, the Collection*. Durham NC: Duke University Press, 1993.

Tagg, John. *The Burden of Representation: Essays on Photographies and Histories*. Minneapolis: University of Minnesota Press, 1993.

Taylor, Colin. *"Ho, for the Great West": The West of William Blackmore*. London: Eatome, 1980.

Trachtenberg, Alan. *Reading American Photographs: Images as History, Mathew Brady to Walker Evans*. New York: Hill & Wang, 1989.

Truettner, William, ed. *The West as America: Reinterpreting Images of the Frontier, 1820–1920*. Washington DC: Smithsonian Institution Press, 1991.

Utley, Robert. *The Lance and the Shield: The Life and Times of Sitting Bull*. New York: Henry Holt, 1993.

Viola, Herman. *Diplomats in Buckskins: A History of Indian Delegations in Washington City*. Washington DC: Smithsonian Institution Press, 1981.

Vizenor, Gerald. *Fugitive Poses: Native American Indian Scenes of Absence and Presence*. Lincoln: University of Nebraska Press, 1998.

Walker, James. *Lakota Belief and Ritual*. Edited by Raymond J. DeMallie and Elaine A. Jahner. Lincoln: University of Nebraska Press, 1980.

———. *Lakota Myth*. Edited by Elaine A. Jahner. Lincoln: University of Nebraska Press, 1983.

———. *Lakota Society.* Edited by Raymond J. DeMallie. Lincoln: University of Nebraska Press, 1982.

Willis, Deborah, ed. *Picturing Us: African-American Identity in Photography.* New York: New Press, 1994.

Wyatt, Victoria. *Images from the Inside Passage: An Alaskan Portrait by Winter and Pond.* Seattle: University of Washington Press, 1989.

———. "Interpreting the Balance of Power: A Case Study of Photographer and Subject in Images of Native Americans." *Exposure* 28 (winter 1991–92): 23–33.

Index

Cancat